Thinking

Edited by **Tony Cotton**

Orders: please contact Bookpoint Ltd, 39 Milton Park, Abingdon, Oxon OX14 4TD. Telephone: (44) 01235 400414, Fax: (44) 01235 400454. Lines are open from 9.00–6.00, Monday to Saturday, with a 24 hour message answering service. Email address: orders@bookpoint.co.uk

British Library Cataloguing in Publication Data
A catalogue record for this title is available from The British Library

ISBN 0 340 70513 2

First published 1998
Impression number   10 9 8 7 6 5 4 3 2 1
Year   2004 2003 2002 2001 2000 1999 1998

Typeset by Fakenham Photosetting Ltd, Fakenham, Norfolk.
Printed in Great Britain for Hodder & Stoughton Educational, a division of Hodder Headline Plc, 338 Euston Road, London NW1 3BH by Redwood Books, Trowbridge, Wiltshire.

Contents

Part 1

Part 2

Part 3

Part 4

Acknowledgements

We must particularly thank Cas who ensured that writing the book was as enjoyable a process for our children as it was for us. Thanks also to Mellor Primary School which provided meeting space and tea and coffee making facilities without which none of this would have been possible. On a personal note, Tony is grateful to Nottingham University for providing him with the time he needed to pull all the pieces of writing together. The photographs were taken by Paul Squires.

Most importantly, we wish to say thank you to all those educators, formal and informal, past and present who have inspired this book.

When we commit ourselves to education as the practice of freedom, we participate in the making of an academic community where we can be and become intellectuals in the fullest and deepest sense of the word. We participate in a way of learning and being that makes the world more rather than less real, one that enables us to live fully and freely. This is the joy in our quest.

bell hooks

For all our children
from
Tony, Helen, Jasbir, Dorothy, Marc, Vicky, Debbion and James

About the Authors

James Burkmar

Since school James has been an active musician, a career he resumed after completing a degree in archaeology at Leicester University. After three years as a session vocalist he returned to Leicester to pursue his own musical interests. Since then he has taught music privately and through workshops, taught in prisons, community studios and worked as a builder, an archaeologist and shopfitter. Currently he is based at a college of further education engaged in development work within the Student Union. He also works for a recording studio and is involved in setting up Youth Training projects, running extracurricular events and planning musical projects of his own.

Tony Cotton

Having gained a degree in mathematics and a PGCE from Sheffield University, Tony taught in secondary schools up to the level of head of department for eight years before moving to The Centre for Multicultural Education in Leicester working as an advisory teacher across all phases of education. During this time he also studied for his MA in education. He then spent time as an advisor to educational publishers. His work includes involvement in the production of an innovative primary mathematics scheme. He is presently a member of the Mathematics Education Team at Nottingham University. He has published books aimed at learners of mathematics as well as for teachers of mathematics. These include *Talking Mathematics, Talking Language* published by the Association of Mathematics Teachers, and *Mathematics Everywhere* published by Collins Educational.

Debbion Currie

Debbion is currently working as a youth worker and as part of a Staff/Student Liaison Team in a busy college of further education in Leicester. She has a degree in performing arts and has taught in both primary and secondary schools. More recently she has performed and directed in her own right in arts events in Leicester and London. She also works regularly on a voluntary basis in her local primary school.

Dorothy Francis

Dorothy worked in various community initiatives including a women's training programme before moving to her present job as business development officer with the Leicester and County Co-operative Development Agency (LCCDA). Dorothy's previous publications include reviews and articles for *Trouble and Strife*, a feminist magazine as well as various other community-based publications. Dorothy has a diploma in Teaching English as a Foreign Language and a diploma from the Institute of Personnel and Development.

Vicky Jones

Vicky has a fine art degree and is an independent film maker. She has run practical workshops in film and video with children and adults of all ages and abilities for 15 years. although she has no formal teaching qualification she has taught in many different locations from village halls to nursery schools, from FE colleges to Arts spaces. Vicky specialises in working with adults with learning disabilities. Recent film projects include *The A–Z of Disability* and *Safety Street*, a training film about personal safety for and by adults with learning disabilities. She is currently working as a film maker in residence developing film projects with groups that are traditionally under-represented in the media community.

Jasbir Mann

After graduating with a degree in psychology and completing her PGCE Jasbir taught in a Bradford community school, then moved to Loughborough to teach in an 11–14 high school. Jasbir spent four years at the Centre for Multicultural Education, first as an advisory teacher for language support and then as an advisory teacher for multicultural education. Now she is the Headteacher at Mellor Community Primary School, one of the largest primary schools in Leicester. Being involved in community education, she is concerned with openness, sharing ownership and empowerment for all involved in education.

Marc McKiernan

Marc attended grammar school and went on to gain a first degree in the arts. His initial career was as a youth worker on adventure playgrounds and in youth clubs. Later, he decided to become a scientist. He worked his way through a science degree as a mature student and a single parent. He completed the degree, a PhD, then took up a post as a research scientist. Becoming disillusioned with the contract research system he went into school teaching, completing his PGCE at age 38. He has run several projects on the public understanding of science, including teaching about genetic engineering in a shopping centre. He is currently head of year at a multicultural inner city comprehensive school.

Helen Toft

Since completing her PGCE at Sheffield University, Helen has worked in a variety of secondary and primary schools as well as being a member of a co-operative business whilst taking a break from teaching. In her present post Helen has returned to specialise in what was originally a subsidiary subject, drama. Her route to this job has included 11 years teaching English with drama, as well as five years' experience in Special Needs support teaching across all subjects in both primary and secondary schools. This breadth of teaching experience, plus her time out of schools, continues to inform her outlook and her classroom practice. Her previous publications include work exploring the use of black American literature in the secondary classroom. She is presently in charge of Drama in an inner city comprehensive school.

Preface

On 19 April 1997 a group of eight educators met together as a large group for the first time. Many of us had met previously, formally and informally, professionally and as friends, but on this occasion we met to begin the project which would lead to this book. Although there had been a clear outline for the activities we would engage in on that first day, we simply talked and listened very hard. It proved to be one of the most important days during our lives in education. Over the following months this book took shape, the collaborative act of writing sharpening our own awareness of what it is to teach and to learn – our hope is that we can share with you some of the excitement and intensity of our belief in education as a force for change both within you and through the children with whom you hope to work.

Tony

What came out of the first writing day for me was the similarity of need in the education system now as when we were at school. I was shocked how the experiences of the group reflect so much the experiences of the young people I come into contact with every day – surely things should have changed for the better by now? Have teachers been recreating themselves as a reflection of their worst experiences rather than their best? As our histories unravelled we discovered shared experiences I would never have imagined, and delighted or grieved about differences usually only touched upon. Few of us had an easy educational or social ride, yet we are the ones working together now to bring about change.

Helen

I was aware in the first meeting of the author group how different my experiences were from the others in the author team. However, now, I am comfortable with this difference. Talking through my experiences did not feel awkward or difficult as I have arrived at a point in my life where I am confident with how I feel and what I do.

Jasbir

"It is easy to forget that different people have very different experiences of school and childhood. It's not at all surprising that even at a meeting such as this, of largely like-minded people, there should be such a massive range of experience. I was struck by how particular individuals, particular teachers, and apparently small events have proved extremely influential to us later on. I was amazed that everyone's experiences were intrinsically interesting to all of us. Although there was a lot of talking there was also a lot of listening.

Marc

"I was amazed that my memories of school were so foggy and only through listening to each other did we begin to see our experiences as being of interest to anyone else. By talking through what it was that made teachers inspiring for us, we can discover what it is that can make us into inspiring teachers.

Vicky

"During that first meeting I found myself initially concentrating on the incidents we were describing, but I quickly moved to wondering why individuals had remembered particular incidents on particular days. What was it that made us tick? What was it that made us register these vitally important moments in our development. On occasions I felt as though I was really there, back in the classroom actively taking part in the memory.

James

"I initially found the first session very painful. It took a long time for me to say anything because I was feeling emotional and vulnerable; I was afraid I would cry if I spoke. I suppose I had suppressed my painful memories of school and relegated them to an experience that ended 20 years ago but which has no bearing on me today. Working on this book has forced me to question this and acknowledge just how much my schooling has affected me and made me the person I am today. It has showed me that there is a possibility for change in our schools and it is that hope which brought us together to write this book.

Dorothy

"I look back on the first session as a semi-therapeutic counselling activity. I felt expected to 'open up' about 'that time' in a very short space of time which was very difficult. However, one anecdote led to another, trains of thought from one person triggering new ideas in another. It was a very confusing, tiring but interesting session. We must not lose sight of these feelings – our learners must have them all the time.

Debbion

Introduction

Many people want to become teachers to change things. Some want to do better than the teachers who taught them. Some remember a teacher or teachers who inspired them, who made them feel confident and comfortable about themselves, who helped them see the sort of person they really are, and who made things possible that otherwise would have seemed impossible. This book contains memories of all sorts of teachers, and how individuals react in many different ways to these teachers.

We hope that the anecdotes and memories offered in this book, along with their commentaries, will support and challenge all those interested in teaching at any level. 'Support' in that you will recognise in the anecdotes experiences of your own. 'Challenge' as you explore the diversity of experience described and analyse it from our own perspective, to arrive at a clearer understanding of how you can draw on your own experience in order to become the sort of teacher you want to be.

The book does not set out simply to offer you tips on how to be a successful teacher, although we hope you will find many useful ideas within its pages. By using extracts from the biographies of a wide range of practising educators we aim to locate learning and teaching within individuals, rather than within particular institutions. In this way the worries you will have about discipline and control, about making your lessons interesting, about whether or not children will like you, can be explored through sharing these anxieties with the authors in their stories. We have all felt this way, we have all had crises of confidence, but through talking, sharing, observing and acting differently have moved towards becoming confident in the many roles we play as educators. We would hope that you will be able to use this book to develop and support your own story within education, and begin to think about what will drive you as a teacher, and how you can best live up to your ambitions.

What makes a 'good' teacher?

Teachers in the state sector of formal education are expected to have certain competencies. This is the way that external bodies describe the skills and attitudes which may be expected in a beginning teacher. Many of these competencies are laid down by the Department of Education, and Teacher Education Institutions have to show evidence that they are helping their students gain these competencies. These requirements can be summarised as follows.

Successful teachers must:
   • understand the subject they are teaching in depth;
   • understand how to use their own knowledge to support pupils' learning of their subject;
   • be able to create a positive atmosphere in their classrooms which encourages learning;
   • be able to judge how well pupils are doing and inform pupils, parents and others about the progress pupils are making;
   • understand the role of education in wider society.

As you will see from Table 1 at the end of this introduction, we have selected anecdotes to illustrate these competencies in practice. We hope this moves away from a dry commentary on the competencies teachers are expected to have, to offer images of how 'competent' teachers operate in real classrooms with real pupils. We have also extended this list of competencies to include further skills which we think 'good' teachers have (Table 2). These can be summarised as:

   • an ability to see the links between different subject areas and draw on these in the classroom;
   • an ability to learn from experience;
   • an ability to use a wide range of techniques in the classroom;
   • an ability to show positive regard and active support to fellow learners and colleagues;
   • an ability to take risks which may lead to innovative ideas;
   • an ability to share goals with learners and colleagues;
   • an ability to allow others to see education as a positive force for change.

Of course 'good' teachers do not exhibit all these characteristics at all times. But when things have gone well, or when we have observed a lesson and been impressed by the teacher, some of these qualities are often present. Neither is the list a checklist of skills to learn. Perhaps it is better seen as the beginning of a reflective conversation with ourselves: 'Am I looking at how my subject can draw on pupils' experiences in other curricular areas?'; 'Am I sharing my goals with the students and colleagues?' and so on.

Much has been written about 'good teaching' over the last few years. Much of it seems prescribed as if there is a perfect model which we can all aim for. As a team of authors we do not believe that we can offer a single view of what it is to be an effective teacher, in fact we do not believe that a single ideal model either exists or should be strived for. Part of the reason for the selection of contributors to this book is to offer as wide a view as possible as to what may make a good teacher. There are many kinds of good teacher. The challenge of this book is to help you recognise the type of good teacher you can become.

Learning from experience

As you will have realised we set great store in learning through our own experiences. This is often described as developing as a 'reflective practitioner'. It is common to find many teaching courses defining one of their main aims as 'developing reflective practitioners'. We have clearly been influenced by this idea as the book consists of 'reflections' both of our own experiences and on what other experiences mean to us.

Reflection can be seen as turning something over in your mind. Not just letting thoughts pass through our minds but consciously 'turning them over' to see if our view develops from giving an incident serious thought. This can help us reformulate our own ideas and our ways of looking at things. It also can help us link different events in our lives and different ideas we have together so that we can see connecting structures within our thoughts and actions. Most importantly, perhaps, reflecting helps us learn how to best use our personal experience to develop in the future. This helps us become more in control of the way in which we think and act. We begin to act in particular ways because we have made a conscious decision to do so, we feel more comfortable about the way we operate and so feel more in control of our lives.

A colleague recently reminded me that the one thing we do not learn from experience is how to learn from experience. The process of thinking carefully about the issues raised by the authors may help you become better equipped to learn from your own experience in the future.

Reflections from the classroom

Reflecting on classroom incidents can help in other ways. It can help us explore the reasons why children behave in particular ways in particular situations. How does the way that we work as teachers produce the particular responses it does from children? An anecdote may challenge something we have previously believed to be true and in this way make us rethink our own ideas. An anecdote can offer us an alternative point of view to an incident. Indeed, the commentaries in the book take on this function. There are always several sides to every story. This form of 'turning over' the story can help us work on our own understanding of incidents in our own lives. The anecdotes present teaching and learning as a human activity. Feelings play a part in all our schooling, and we need to find ways of working with these feelings as we develop as teachers. Using anecdotes helps us in our own hypothesising – it helps us ask the question, 'What would I have done?' and more importantly, 'Why would I have done it like that?' The questions at the end of each chapter are designed to support you in this process of questioning.

Keeping a journal

In many ways this book could be seen as extracts from our journals over a shared 250 years in education. We hope that you will begin this process of journal writing whilst you read this book or perhaps use the book to add to a journal you already keep. I know it seems like hard work but as the book is all about thinking over what it is that has made us into the kinds of educators we are, we want you to join us in thinking about what kind of teacher you may turn out to be. It may pay off for several reasons.

Writing helps you learn because in committing something to the page you have to think about it in a different way. In some ways you have to believe in what you write and give your thoughts more attention than if you leave them unwritten. It also allows you to come back to these thoughts at a later date, re-examine them and see if you still think in the same way. This may be embarrassing sometimes, but it is always useful to look back on the way we used to think and compare it to how we think now.

More pragmatically, for those readers about to embark on a teaching course it is very likely that you will be asked to keep a journal of your experiences in school. You will be asked by your tutors to 'reflect' on your experiences in school, to analyse your actions, to offer alternative interpretations to the observations you have made in school. This is a skill to be learnt and developed as you move through your course and through your teaching career. We hope that by using this book before you embark on your course, or as a part of your course, we will support you in developing these skills. For others who have a more general interest in education we would encourage you to start a journal as you read the book. At the end of each chapter there are questions to ask yourself. Through writing responses to these questions you may find it more easy to uncover what you 'actually' think about teaching and learning. So, buy yourself a nice book with blank pages, find a pen that you enjoy writing with, make writing a pleasure and you are ready to begin.

Working with colleagues

We do not believe that reflection is something that you always do on your own in a quiet place, although making time and space to think is obviously important.

Through the process of writing this book we have been reminded that often the most powerful form of reflection can happen through collaborative activity. The process of talking with others about our thoughts and feelings encouraged us to unravel why it is we think in the way that we do. We had to decide why certain memories are more significant than others, why certain experiences seem important whilst others do not. So we would also encourage you to share this book with a friend or other students on your course. Read chapters together and see if your interpretations match – if they do, why do they? If they don't, what can account for the differences? In this way you may also begin to become more involved with the authors. More importantly you may begin to uncover things in your own mind which will help you learn more about yourself as a teacher.

What is in the book?

The book opens with a series of personal statements from the author team. Our aim is that these statements will introduce you to our personal educational philosophies and beliefs. After reading these introductions you may feel as though you share a background or a philosophy with a particular author and focus on their memories as you read the book. Alternatively, you may enjoy seeing how authors with contrasting backgrounds describe their experiences. However you choose to read the book, we certainly hope you will enjoy seeing at which stages we agree or disagree on the issues we are discussing.

Of course, any process which involves looking back to see what has influenced us in the past must also contain hopes for the future and an outline of where we are at the moment. We hope to encourage you, the reader, to become involved with the book from this early stage too in assessing your own personal starting points.

The personal statements are followed by a series of anecdotes drawn from experience of teaching in a wide range of contexts, from university education departments, across primary and secondary schools, into the further education sector including work with adults and children with learning difficulties, through to business training and work in the creative arts. Through conversations we have realised how we have all been affected by certain events during our own experiences in education which have led us to adopt certain styles in our own work. There are memories of ourselves as learners, memories of colleagues who have greatly influenced the ways that we presently work, experiences of our own children in schools as well as our reactions to the experiences of others. Each chapter concludes with questions for you to work on for yourself. These questions could form the basis of your personal journal mentioned earlier.

The first set of anecdotes focus on individual memories of the authors from their time in education. These chapters focus on key moments which made us aware of how we learnt within school, or how we were hindered from learning. Many of these 'critical incidents' have had a lasting impact on the way in which we view education today, and the ways in which we work with our learners. A brief introduction points out some of the key issues raised in this section. The main aim of the section is to introduce you to the authors in the hope that you share some of their experiences. We would also hope that reading these experiences will spark memories of your own from your time in school. The three chapters here describe both our most inspirational teachers and those who we would rather forget. There are also anecdotes from those critical moments when teachers attempted to offer us advice for our future – sometimes supportive and sometimes devastatingly undermining our ambitions.

The next two chapters focus both on colleagues we have observed who have most influenced our own practice, and teaching sessions of our own which have proved memorable. We reflect on the ways in which we have altered our own practices as a result of these experiences. We also emphasise how teachers in all forms of education can learn from experiences in contexts which at first seem far removed from the situation in which they are presently working. Within these accounts is also a discussion of how we measure success within our different fields, what makes a session successful for us? How do we measure this success from the point of view of the learners we are working with?

The final chapter offers you our shared vision of what it is to be an educated person, what sort of skills may be required of teachers who have taught such an 'educated' person, and finally a vision of the school in which these teachers ply their trade. The conclusion is a joint statement outlining our beliefs in education and our hopes for the future of education in the broadest sense. The conclusion arises as a result of the collaborative endeavour which we have undertaken in writing this book and in many senses is our own reflective response to the process we have shared.

How to use the book

You will be able to use the book in many ways. A skim through the following pages will allow you to focus on particular topics of interest or on your 'key author' and is probably a good way to start. Of course, the first place to go is our own introductions – in this way you can decide exactly who you want to track through the book.

If you are interested in developing a particular competency or find yourself particularly nervous about an aspect of teaching, you may find Tables 1 and 2 useful. These tables list the competencies we described earlier. Table 1 consists of the 'official' Department for Education competencies and Table 2 of the additional competencies we have suggested. These tables show you the page numbers where you can find examples of these competencies in practice.

Finally, you may be interested in a particular issue, or a particular context for teaching and learning. Table 3 offers an overview of all the anecdotes from all the authors, together with the situation the anecdote describes and the key issues we feel the anecdote raises. This table may also be useful in enabling you to return to a particular anecdote when you wish to reread sections of the book.

If you are working or reading as a group you may all find it valuable to read one particular anecdote, perhaps selected as it discusses a particular key issue for you, or takes place in a setting which mirrors your own. After individually reading the anecdote, talk through the key issues it raises for each of you. Does it remind you of any memories of your own? In this way you mimic the process of writing the book and can perhaps uncover important experiences of your own to build on.

Table 1: Teaching competencies

Teachers should be able to:	Page number
understand the subject they are teaching.	37, 40, 74, 75, 76, 78, 80, 82, 93
understand how to use their own knowledge to support pupils' learning of their subject.	31, 40, 74, 75, 76, 78, 80, 82, 93, 97
be able to create a positive atmosphere in their classrooms which encourages learning.	31, 34, 35, 37, 45, 47, 50, 58, 73, 74, 75, 76, 78, 82, 83, 88, 91, 93, 96
be able to judge how well pupils are doing and inform pupils, parents and others about the progress pupils are making.	40, 51, 57, 58, 62, 76, 78, 93, 104
understand the role of education in a wider society.	34, 36, 39, 51, 54, 58, 63, 81, 83, 91, 95, 99, 102

Table 2: Further competencies

Teachers should have:	Page number
an ability to see the links between different subject areas and draw on these in the classroom.	34, 37, 78, 80, 81, 83, 93
an ability to learn from experience.	31, 71, 73, 88, 93, 99, 103
an ability to use a wide range of techniques in the classroom.	34, 74, 75, 82, 83, 88, 95, 97
an ability to show positive regard and active support to fellow learners and colleagues.	35, 39, 47, 50, 57, 58, 73, 78, 81, 83, 91, 96, 98
an ability to take risks which may lead to innovative ideas.	34, 35, 74, 75, 76, 81, 83, 88, 93, 95, 98
an ability to share goals with learners and colleagues.	36, 40, 47, 48, 73, 81, 83, 96, 102
an ability to allow others to see education as a positive force for change.	31, 39, 57, 58, 81, 83, 91, 99, 102

Table 3: Contexts and Issues

Chapter 2	Our Best Teachers	
Author	*Context*	*Issues*
Marc	Chemistry lectures at University.	Creating subject relevance.
James	English at secondary school.	Giving pupils a voice in lessons.
Debbion	History teaching and informal education.	High expectations. Positive encouragement.
Helen	English teaching.	Personal connections with teacher. Taking risks in lessons.
Jasbir	Asian girl in all-white school. PE lessons.	Home/school contact. Valuing individual experience and skills from home.
Vicky	Strong women as role models.	Teachers as individuals with lives outside school.
Dorothy	Informal contact with educator after leaving school.	High expectations giving confidence. Challenging institutional prejudice.
Tony	Piano lessons.	Enthusiasm and commitment to subject for its own sake. High expectation.

Chapter 3 Why do they think we ever forget?

Author	Context	Issues
Helen	Spellings in primary school.	Public humiliation of pupils.
James	Working-class boy in grammar school.	Bullying teachers. Ritual humiliation.
Jasbir	Choosing pupils for school performance.	Favouritism.
Tony	Primary reading scheme. Setting in mathematics. Son in primary school	Petty application of rules and policies.
Marc	Secondary Latin lessons.	Questioning to humiliate pupils.
Vicky	Pupils bullying her child.	Teachers recognising and dealing with problems.

Chapter 4   Careers Advice

Author	Context	Issues
Dorothy	Careers interview in school.	Inequality of advice through discriminatory practice and beliefs.
Helen	Post 'A' level interview with deputy head.	School control over individual career choice.
Tony	'A' level choices.	Expectations and gender.
Vicky	Informal careers advice.	School ignoring responsibility for future development of pupils.
Marc	Meeting ex-pupil out of school.	High expectations of behaviour.

Chapter 5   Expectations and Motivation

Author	Context	Issues
Jasbir	Parental expectations.	Schools being clear about explaining success and failure to parents and pupils. Alienation from system which does not accept difference.
Dorothy	Motivation from mother.	Importance of belief in learners from school. Impact of racism on self-esteem and learning.
James	Alienated group within school.	Peer group pressure. Alienated individuals forming identities in school. Positive role of peer groupings.
Helen	Home and school expectations clashing.	Academic success challenging community expectations.
Tony	Pupils challenging system.	Pupil/teacher control and power.

Chapter 6   Watching others teach

Author	Context	Issues
Tony	Staffroom conversations. Art class. Mathematics class.	Positive regard for pupils. High expectations and non-patronising approach.
Marc	Secondary science teacher education.	Individual needs and pupil responsibility. Deep knowledge of and enthusiasm for your subject.
Dorothy	Adult training.	Fitting teaching to individual needs. Displaying enthusiasm for your subject.
Jasbir	11–14 high school.	Thematic approaches to curriculum. Learning from colleagues. Cultural awareness.
Vicky	Science in the community. Film/Video workshops with learners with special needs.	Encouraging involvement of all participants. High expectations.
Helen	School Council training for pupils.	Collaborative teaching. High expectations.

Chapter 7   Our best lessons

Author	Context	Issues
Marc	Comparison of two lessons: one with group of low-attaining GCSE students and one as tutor of Open University group.	Motivation of students with low self-esteem. Strategies for coping with disruptive learners.
Dorothy	Training a group of women. TEFL sessions.	How to tackle controversial issues with groups. Challenging racist behaviour. High expectations and relevance of subject matter.
Helen	School performance.	How to learn from and with colleagues and students. Valuing difference.
Vicky	Working with adults with learning difficulties.	Being aware of specific needs of a group.
Debbion	Theatre work. FE college common room.	Group responsibility for learning process. Challenging inappropriate institutionalised behaviour.
Tony	Primary mathematics.	What do pupils value as good lessons?
Jasbir	Being a primary headteacher.	Expectations of self and others. Communication in schools.

Part 1

WHERE ARE WE STARTING FROM?

Chapter 1

Introducing the Authors

Introduction

Whenever starting work with a new group of learners it is important to quickly establish a feeling of trust. The group need to know where you, the teacher, are coming from at the very beginning of this relationship so that they get a feeling for what to expect as they work with you. In a similar way, as a group of writers we needed to find out early in the process what values we shared and what made us different. What follows is the result of this process. We hope that you find one or two of us to connect with. As you read through you may want to underline things that strike you as particularly relevant to your own experience (unless of course you have borrowed this book from a library!).

Jasbir

Who are you?

I am Jasbir Mann. I am a headteacher who enjoys working with people – children and adults. I am Raj and Balroop's mum and am married to Ranjit, who is a pharmacist. I am a British Sikh born in Bradford. I am efficient, organised and enjoy my work. I am healthy, most of the time! I enjoy keeping fit. I hope I am approachable and keen to develop new ideas and approaches in my work. I am an optimist.

Why did you choose to be this?

I didn't plan my career. Opportunities arose and if they felt right or exciting I took them. I had never planned to be a headteacher but when the vacancy arose I knew I had the vision and creativity to make the school successful. The job has now given me many chances to become involved in doing the things I enjoy doing.

What has influenced you to take this direction in life?
My family from an early age had high expectations of me. I had to do well educationally. The push and encouragement came mainly from them. My family saw education as the only way to gain equality in this society.

What were the most meaningful parts of your education?
I enjoyed going to school. It gave me the freedom to do things my friends took for granted.

In what ways does education fit in with the values held at home?
I knew my alphabet and had basic number skills before I started school. At home there is a belief that learning is a life-long process, you never stop learning. I have always been taught to respect all points of view, especially those of people who are older and have experience of life. We were taught that education leads to a better quality of life, not just through individuals achieving but through an increased social standing of the family.

Why do you continue to be involved in education?
Because I enjoy working with children. Most days I get tremendous job satisfaction.

What are your strengths as an educator?
An ability to listen, motivate and lead by example. I like to be questioned in what I am doing.

What would you change about the way you work?
At times I need to say no. I have a tendency to be involved in too many things – both in work and outside.

What/who influences your work now?
Colleagues in and outside school. My children and my family. Attending conferences and reading books on all aspects of education.

What are the biggest frustrations?
Mainly external pressures such as the budget constraints on school resources and staffing which effect decisions that should be purely educational. Visits from school inspectors are also more stressful than useful. Disillusioned staff and staff who do not seem prepared to learn particularly depress me.

The greatest joys and satisfactions?
My own children doing well and being able to make choices. Children who leave school and want to return. Children who used to hate school enjoying attending. Aggressive and abusive parents eventually supporting the school. Racist parents being challenged by their own children. Getting my own way!!

What hopes do you have for the people you work with?
That they enjoy their jobs and continue to learn and develop. That they continually question their own and children's views. That they stop moaning. That they feel valued. That we work as a team.

What are your hopes for the future?
To meet all my deadlines. To finish my MEd, to continue to find my work interesting, to know when it is the right time to move on, to be more involved with the media, to inspire others, to be the Head of a Centre of Excellence.

James

Who are you?
I am James Burkmar. I'm 35 and I describe myself as a musician/writer as well as a parent/husband. In my professional life I am a development worker and manager working in a student union at a further education college. My particular role is in access work.

Why did you choose to be this?
I am a musician and husband for the love of it, a parent by accident and for the love of it. I became a development worker and manager because I can do it, I make money at it and some areas of the work are very enjoyable.

What has influenced you to take this direction in life?
As far as music and writing go, I'm not sure. I always wanted to play/ compose. I had one really good English literature teacher who inspired me to read and write for myself. Later, family life kind of caught up with me although I had always seen myself with kids. I have always organised things – when I was ten I arranged a charity football match, so perhaps that was my first development project.

What were the most meaningful parts of your education?
My dad – 'Be detailed, be thorough, be honest and don't be flaky!'
Conversations with relatives – 'Be yourself', 'Reach and go for it.'
School organised my approach to working, being able to work, apply myself, self-discipline, and so on. My peer group as a teenager. I had to find ways of being a part of something whilst retaining my individuality. I think football taught me the same things as well as allowing for self-expression.

In what ways does education fit in with the values held at home?
The work ethic, a sharing, learning community and the simple idea of a fair chance.

Why do you continue to be involved in education?
Because it allows me to make money and it is something I *can* do. In my own area of work there is a lot of room for manoeuvre so that I can *participate* as well as lead or teach/tutor.

What are your strengths as an educator?
I can motivate. I'm thorough. I am a good researcher and try hard to see things through to the end. I care about people and their situations.

What would you change about the way you work?
I would improve my time management. My lack of time management skills can be very damaging!

What/who influences your work now?
My wife. Particular friends and colleagues as well as my personal ambition and motivation. There are also negative things (from the political to the personal) in terms of motivating me to fight against them.

What are the biggest challenges you face?

Overcoming personal prejudices and fears and negativity. Not being lazy – re-evaluating what I am doing, not being complacent.

The greatest joys and satisfactions?

My kids, my love, our and my adventures. Music in all its forms within my life, still being 'out there' and asked to do things.

What hopes do you have for the people you work with?

That they look after themselves physically/mentally/spiritually. That they stay happy and balance this with a sense of direction, self-government and ambition.

Can you describe the social contexts in which you work?

An FE college funded by FEFC and legislated by Acts of Parliament. A wide variety of students/customers: young/mature, Black/Asian/White, male/female. Different courses, different class backgrounds.

How do these factors affect your work?

A great deal. The development of provisions and support has to be pitched in varying degrees to different people and groups of people. All have different struggles. This factor is present all the time, every day.

What are your hopes for the future?

To retain and build on my creativity. To retain and build on my family. To travel and to stay healthy.

Tony

Who are you?

I am someone who has a belief that education can change the world for the better. I am a teacher, an educator in the broadest sense, I am a father and a son. Music is extremely important to me both to listen to and to make. I often see myself as a frustrated performer and wonder if the reason I became a teacher was to satisfy my need to stand up and 'perform'.

Why did you choose to be this?

I'm not sure how much choice I feel as though I had. The more I find out about my family history, the more it feels as though I am following a very long line of footsteps, not just as a teacher but in the beliefs I hold about education. When I finished university it was a very pragmatic choice to do a teaching year – I knew I didn't want to work in 'industry', whatever that meant, and my girlfriend at the time said, 'Why don't you be a teacher – I think you would be good at it.' So I took her advice.

What has influenced our direction in life?

My family and close friends as well as my political beliefs. I also had a clear idea of what I didn't want to do. I didn't want to be a headteacher. I didn't want to be tied down to the same school for too long and I enjoy change. Very special colleagues in several places have shown me the way that I want to work and I have looked for places where I can work in the way I want to.

What were the most meaningful parts of your own education?

Reading has always been the way that I learn. Maybe this seems strange for someone who has become a mathematician. I still learn most through reading as well as through working with other people. I feel as though my education started in earnest once I finished with formal education at 21.

In what ways does education fit in with the values held at home?

As I think back over my childhood I suppose education has always been valued. My mother became a teacher during my time at secondary school. This involved starting with O levels and A levels after having her family. My dad is still one of the most important teachers in my life, although he was a design engineer by trade. I share my house with another teacher, the best teacher I have ever worked with and someone who is a huge influence on the way I work, so I cannot separate education from home.

Why do you continue to be involved in education?
Because I think it is the main hope for the future. I honestly believe that through education we can enable our children to work for a better world – whatever that may look like. I also still get a real buzz from teaching and getting feedback from students of all ages about sessions that I run, whether teaching 11-year-olds mathematics or postgraduate students about educational theory and practice.

What are your strengths as an educator?
I am told I am enthusiastic, I think people enjoy the fact that I don't put on an act. When I teach I am exactly the same person as when I am not teaching. Hopefully that means people know where they stand with me.

What would you change about the way you work?
I tend to have too many things on the go at the same time. I am good at having ideas but never seem to have the time to finish them all off, so I end up writing interminable lists in an effort to see how I might fit everything in.

What are the biggest challenges you face?
External constraints, whether they be government restrictions on curriculum, or others' common-sense ideas of how you should work in classrooms which often seem to stifle creativity.

What/who influences your work now?
Conversations with the people I work with at the university and with the students; having my own ideas challenged makes me think hard about how I work. However, the greatest influences will always be the children I work with in schools.

What are the greatest joys and satisfactions?
People responding positively to things I have to say or things I try out. Students in school who clearly have been challenged by the work we are doing but have enjoyed the challenge.

What hopes do you have for the people you work with?
That they feel as though they are in control of their own lives. That they can make decisions which will help them live the sort of lives they want to live and challenge those things which get in the way. One of the books I read in my first year of teaching suggested that the aim of schooling should be to equip all kids with a built-in crap-detector – that still feels like a good aim.

How would you describe the people you work with?

I couldn't pigeonhole. I work with student teachers, teachers beginning and experienced, pupils of all ages. The people I most enjoy working with are teachers who are excited about working with all children, and learners who question me about what I am doing.

Do you work with other educators outside the workplace?

I don't feel as though I am at work only when I am in the university. It seems as though I have important conversations about education in many places – front rooms, pubs, seminar rooms and, of course, schools. So I feel as though I am around educators, in the broadest sense, for most of my waking hours. It is very difficult for me to see myself as having a working life and a separate sort of 'other' life.

Can you describe the contexts in which you work?

Occasionally I feel embattled by external constraints due to funding or legislation but I am becoming better at focusing on what is possible rather than the problems. I much prefer to work in schools which may be described by others as 'inner city' or 'deprived'. They don't feel 'deprived' to me as I come across the most creative people imaginable in these situations.

How do these contexts affect your work?

They cause me to be creative and flexible even though occasionally I may stamp my feet in frustration.

What are your hopes for the future?

I don't really know what the future brings. I am actually quite happy working in the present and waiting to see what challenges the future will bring

Debbion

Who are you?

I am 33, female, black, a mother, wife, writer, youth worker, performer, director and community worker.

Why did you choose to be this?

Because they were things I was good at and I couldn't settle on any one 'career'. I think I purposefully drifted (if you can do that?).

What has influenced you to take this direction in life?

I don't think there is anything more important than being creative. Being creative is about empowerment. We *are* created – therefore we owe it to ourselves to become creative. Through the work I do, be it community or performance work, I aim to empower people to become creative themselves.

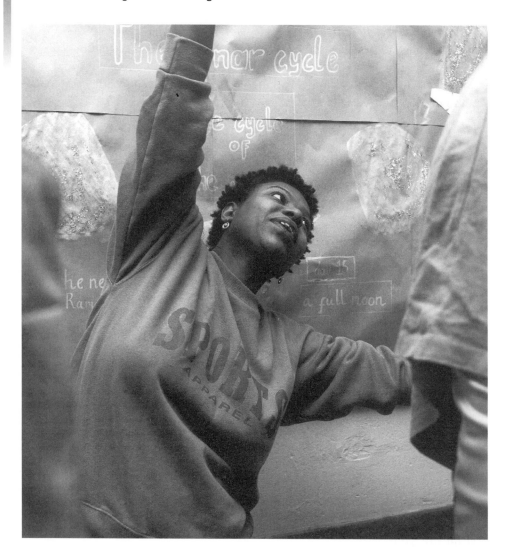

That seems to be what it's all about – helping people look at things differently, and seeing things differently yourself as a part of the process.

What were the most meaningful parts of your education?

An A level sociology course at college with a Jewish tutor. I learnt why I was the way I was, how I fitted into society. I understood where I was in terms of sex, race and class. Why I was in my position with all its limitations. I learnt to forgive myself for my perceived failure through understanding my position better.

In what ways does education fit in with values held at home?

Education mirrored the values at home which were held by my parents.

Education had a real importance in principle but nobody really understood how it worked in practice.

Why do you continue to be involved in education?

Because I believe that everyone is involved in education anyway. We are all involved in education whether as a mother at home or in any other role. I have the ability to recognise the value of informal education.

What are your strengths as an educator?

The ability to understand someone else's perspective by relating to it or because it mirrors my own experience.

What would you change about the way you work?

More time to focus on myself so that I could do more training for myself. I could then give this back to others through my work.

What are the biggest challenges you face?

My main challenge is myself. My fears and insecurities hold me back and I have to continually work through them. Being a mother, I don't always have the time to be fully creative in everything from mothering to performing.

What are your greatest joys and satisfactions?

My greatest satisfaction is knowing that I can have my cake and eat it because I made the cake. The ingredients of the cake are children, husband, work, performing, friends and travel.

What hopes do you have for the people you work with?

It is important to me that I actively want people to be happy in whatever decisions they take about their lives. Having had tutors who seemed to want to destroy people's self-confidence and motivation, I want to see people who can work with multiple choices and multiple outcomes in all areas of education. I do not believe there must be a set pattern to our lives.

What are your hopes for the future?

I would like to spend more time at home consolidating my creative energy. I need to slow down and work out what I want to do next. I would like to take a piece I have just directed abroad while I am pregnant and still have the energy.

Marc

Who are you?

A teacher, a school teacher, a science explainer, a parent persuader (with my Head of Year hat on), a planner and improver of whole school issues.

Why did you choose to be this?

I like the hurly burly of schools, having to do several things at once. I wanted a career change which would put me in a position where I could influence the environment in which I worked. I felt rather powerless before entering school teaching. I like the opportunities to be resourceful. Children are ever refreshing to work with. I like the sense of community within a school.

What has influenced you to take this direction in life?

Recently I wanted to have greater control over what happened to me, and to have more influence, for instance with parents as a Head of Year. I also have a wish to see science as a more central part of schooling, a much more far-reaching part of the school curriculum. I see science as a skill base for the whole school. I also wonder whether I have an intrinsic need for periodic change? I like schools because there are opportunities to do this.

What were the most meaningful parts of your education?

Learning to draw. Being shown how to enjoy the English language, including how to take it to pieces at an early age. Latin (this is not a misprint)! Science *after* I left school, with the exception of a practical, process–based science scheme when I was at school. Playing in school sports teams; if I had to choose, this would probably be top of the list.

In what ways does education fit in with values held at home?

I grew up with the idea that anything was possible and that knowledge and skills open doors. Information handling was very important. There was an appreciation of these widely applicable skills which was partly contradicted by what I now see as an over-reverence for experts. Things didn't necessarily have to have an obviously educational purpose. I remember a long car journey as a teenager with my dad when we listened to someone talking for an hour about ancient Spanish organs. We didn't like organs, churches, or the music but we loved the expertise. The speaker was not concerned to tell us anything, he knew *he* was interested, but we could certainly listen if we wanted to. We referred to the talk for the rest of my dad's life as a shorthand for this kind of knowledge and understanding.

Why do you continue to be involved in education?

So I can have a say in what I do. So I can make a difference. I enjoy change. I like to work with a lot of people at once, although I only realised this recently.

What are your strengths as an educator?

An ability to make ideas relevant. My persistence. An ability to pitch things at the right level. I think I have and can implement good teaching ideas quickly. I am not afraid to take risks. I think this is one sign of good teaching.

What would you change about the way you work?

I would like more time, although I am not sure if I would actually plan any better. I am trying to work on the idea of having different kinds of time in school. Particularly as Head of Year this is important, both for myself and my effectiveness, as well as for the way children perceive me. I have to be seen as giving undivided attention.

What/who influences the way you work now?

In science, reading new and sometimes very old books. At work there are whole school pressures to improve our school. The Inspection tail wagging the school dog has definitely resulted in less interesting work by me over the 18 months. My partner influences me as do other teachers I respect, this influence coming from reading their ideas or watching them in action. I am also influenced by specific children. The recognition that I have not enabled a particular child to understand something or gain a skill provides the clearest immediate focus for informing the way I work on a regular basis. The conversations I have with children about their learning which arise from this are also very important.

What are the biggest challenges you face?

Making our school be *perceived* as successful.

What are your biggest frustrations?
Other teachers' low expectations of children.

What are your greatest joys and satisfactions?
Good work from students, a colleague's eyes suddenly opened, students previously seen as 'naughty' being taken seriously by all staff because of my work with the student and often their parents.

What hopes do you have for the people you work with?
To have the students realise they have the choice of leaving the area in which they live. For them to have a more constructively critical view of the world they live in. For them to taken control of their lives. For them to shake off their parents' preconceptions and prejudices.

How would you describe the people you work with?
The students seem to have narrower viewpoints, are less adventurers, are less skilled socially and otherwise, have less trust in education and are more defensive than many other groups of teenagers I have worked with. My teacher colleagues surprisingly fit the same categories, although some of them are extremely clever, perceptive and effective people. Of course, these are generalisations. There are wonderful exceptions both in colleagues and in students.

Do you work with other educators outside your immediate workplace?
I work with my partner doing film/animation/video workshops and on public understanding of science workshops. We want to work together more.

Can you describe the contexts in which you work?
The students' families often suffer high unemployment, low income, low skills level and many have low expectations of education. Fortunately, some of them have a much higher expectation of education. I am working in the aftermath of the education reform maelstrom, and I have no confidence that we are at the end of that. It remains to be seen whether all the reform is educationally sound or not. There are many false comparisons being made with previous regimes, for example the 'trendy 60s'. This is often supported (or unsupported) by poor data.

How do these contexts affect your work?
I have to build opportunities for a success that really is a new idea for many. This has to be balanced with communicating the realities of what happens to students who leave school with few or no skills and qualifications. This is very different to the situation their parents faced when they left school. I began teaching during National Curriculum implementation and so do not find it as threatening as some colleagues, however, clearly reform stated well before the

National Curriculum. No one has ever said that readers should not constantly review their practice, and good teachers always have.

What are your hopes for the future?
To teach exciting science lessons. To alter and widen my students' expectations. To see my current school perceived as successful by all its local community. To climb the career tree in school. I did not want to do this when I entered teaching, but I do now.

Dorothy

Who are you?
I am Dorothy Francis, a mother and teacher at home and a business adviser and teacher at work. I am also a teacher of English as a Foreign Language, a personnel officer, a lapsed sportswoman, an avid reader, a keen cook, a perpetual student and a counsellor.

Why did you choose to be this?
I'm not sure how much of this I chose and how much of it chose me. My working life has been shaped by the educational choices I made, although these choices were made for me to some extent. I was 'not good' at maths and

sciences at school but excelled at English, history, geography and similar subjects. I was not encouraged to do better at maths and science and so I concentrated on the subjects I enjoyed, especially English. I eventually did an English degree and a few years later a TEFL diploma as a follow on.

My job at the Co-operative Development Agency includes a lot of personnel-type work in which I became increasingly interested. I felt that it would be useful to gain a qualification in this area and so pursued a part-time course to obtain my diploma from the Institute of Personnel and Development.

What has influenced you to take this direction in life?

I have worked in community groups or co-operatives for the past 14 years. I enjoy working in this way because I like working with people in a collective manner. Working in a co-operative offers the chance to pursue individual aims within group objectives – to be independent to some extent whilst still receiving support from other group members. I chose to work in this way as I was not happy with the conventional hierarchical methods of working that I had previously experienced.

I like my work because it is about teaching people to help themselves. We train and equip people for business. We work on the principle of teaching people to fish so that they can be self-sustaining rather than giving them the fish so that they can eat for a day. Sometimes it is difficult to let go but the satisfaction and the reward is in seeing a well-run, viable business that you helped to develop.

What were the most meaningful parts of your education?

Learning to read. I had come to this country as a five-year-old and had to contend with many things from racism to the weather. I recall that learning to read was a long and difficult process which I did not enjoy. However, one day it all fell into place and I realised that I could read. I can still remember the moment when, metaphorically speaking, the sun broke through the clouds and the words on the page made sense. Learning to read was a major breakthrough and I soon developed an insatiable appetite, devouring the whole of our class library in a very short time before starting on the school library. At age eight my teacher called my mother to the school and said I should be prevented from reading as it was taking over my life and preventing me from doing my lessons and socialising. He was right but I didn't think so at the time. I felt like a junkie cut off from my fix and would sneak little bits of reading whenever I could, even reading the cornflakes packet.

A positive memory from my time in secondary school is the respect I gained from excelling in sprint track events which helped shore me up through many miserable and depressing times. The other important phase of my education was finally leaving school and going to college. I suddenly had control over my own education and was treated as an adult. This significantly altered my attitude towards education as it meant that I had to take responsibility for my own learning.

In what ways does education fit in with the values held at home?

Education was very important in our home. My mother saw it as a key to a better life and her main aim in life was to ensure that we were well educated and able to earn a living of our own accord. She always allowed us time to do our homework and encouraged us to do better. She taught us basic reading, writing and numeracy skills before we started school and helped us with our work in the early years of schooling. However, she left school herself aged 14 and had not received any education since then, so was not able to help us as much when we got older. Also the methods were so very different from what she remembered.

Why do you continue to be involved in education?

I am in education because I like to teach. I like to share, to see people grow in confidence, skills and knowledge and to know that I was involved in that development. I particularly like working with people in attitude-changing situations as I find this challenging. I also always see myself as involved in education, in that I am constantly learning and love to learn.

What are your strengths as an educator?

I am approachable and although I like to share knowledge I will admit it when I don't know something. I enjoy teaching the subjects that I teach. I remember what it was like not to know, which helps me to avoid patronising my trainees. I recognise the skills that trainees have and use these to help them teach themselves. My style is informal.

What would you change about the way you work?

I use stories and anecdotes a lot in my teaching and this can annoy people who are not used to this method of delivery.

What/who influences your work now?

Past experience, especially past training sessions. I try to remember and replicate good teaching experiences and avoid bad ones. I also think of all the good teachers I have had and try to isolate what made them good in an effort to apply these techniques to my own style.

What are the biggest challenges you face?

Teaching people to run their own businesses when they have no experience in this area. Working with people who left school many years ago and have not been involved in formal education since.

What are your biggest frustrations?

Working with people who don't really want to learn but are there because they have to be or because they don't see any other choice. An example is people who have been unemployed for a long time and feel that running their own business will be the answer, even though they do not have a viable business idea or an aptitude for business. Or people who have decided to set up their own business as a response to a Restart Interview but are not really interested in working for themselves. What they really want is a job and so they are not interested in what I am teaching.

What are your greatest joys and satisfactions?

Seeing the look on people's faces when they realise they can do it (whatever 'it' is) or on realising they understand a term or a concept. Seeing people stand on their own two feet without me because they have learnt all I can teach them.

What hopes do you have for the people you work with?

That they will obtain the skills they need to run their business effectively. That they will feel able to question if they do not understand. That they will learn to question prejudice, discrimination and assumptions.

How would you describe the people you work with?

Most of my clients (they are clients rather than trainees) are aged 25 and above. Our clients usually approach the CDA because they want to set up their own business and need advice, support, training or all three in order to do so. This makes our job easier as they have already identified a learning gap and are prepared to take steps to fill it. My colleagues have all been involved in running their own businesses and so bring this perspective to their work. We tend to share similar views regarding the delivery of our training and others services.

Do you work with other educators outside your workplace?

Not in the formal sense. A good friend and I often discuss our work, especially if we are having problems. She is a trainer and counsellor and our work overlaps in some areas. We learn a lot from each other but have never worked together. The same applies to another friend who works for the Youth Education section of the local council. We have spent many hours over the years discussing good practice and other issues.

My children are great educators and have often caused me to change my viewpoint or my way of working with them through their comments or reactions.

Can you describe the contexts in which you work?

Some clients have strong social, political, ethical reasons for wishing to establish a co-operative, others simply wish to set up in business and have chosen a co-operative approach. However, some of the people who approach us do so as a last resort. About half of our clients are unemployed and are seeking to create their own work. The rest are already in employment but wish to leave this to work for themselves or want to convert this business to a co-operative. The co-op ethos teaches the value of group working, education for all, social responsibility and a fair distribution of profits. The Agency targets groups of people who are perhaps not traditionally (in this country) involved in business. This includes black people, working-class people, the long-term unemployed, women, older people, people with disabilities, lesbians and gay men.

How do these factors affect your work?

It is not possible to teach a defined text, you have to be aware of the group you are talking to and take differences into consideration. Sometimes there is a need to change the lesson plan during a session to take into account factors or issues which have arisen, and so I need to be adaptable.

What are your hopes for the future?

I hope to continue my involvement in teaching. To continue learning and developing. To see teaching of children elevated to the position it deserves. To be more involved in the teaching of my own children.

Vicky

Who are you?

I am a film maker, a mother, a workshop leader, an artist, a technician sometimes and a film practitioner. I specialise in working with adults with disabilities.

Why did you choose to be this?

I'm not sure I exactly *chose* to be this. It was more a matter of doing what I wanted to do and experimenting with ideas related to film. Opportunities to run workshops arose out of all this and it seemed a very natural progression as well as a way of earning money.

What has influenced you to take this direction in life?

I don't remember taking a huge interest in my dad's Standard 8 home movies or even my grandmother's home movies of the 1930s and 1940s, but these must have been an influence I suppose. My fine art degree was one of the few experimental mixed media course in the country at the time and this sent me down a path that I have not really strayed from. It enabled me to not *be* any

one particular thing like a painter or a sculptor. I needed that freedom and I don't feel as though I have changed much since then.

What were the most meaningful parts of your education?
Learning to see through going to Art School. Although on the whole education has only really become meaningful to me recently.

In what ways does education fit in with the values held at home?
Education is an intrinsic part of my current home, I cannot separate the two. My partner is a natural at communicating ideas and my children keep me feeling enthusiastic about their education as I watch them trying to make sense of the world.

Why do you continue to be involved in education?
Because I continue to learn new things myself every day and I still want to inspire others to create their own work. Education improves everybody's quality and understanding of life and gives us hope for the future.

What are your strengths?
I feel very enthusiastic, my approach to working with people has to be fun, informal, fresh and resourceful. I cannot imagine it being any other way.

What/who influences your work now?

Many things – my partner, my children, the interests of the group I am working with, objects, images and sounds I come across in my everyday life, old books on cinematography, watching, reading and talking about other people's approaches to their work.

What are your biggest frustrations?

There is never enough time, so often the final results are not as good as I had hoped. I would like more time to make my own films.

What are your greatest joys and satisfactions?

The magic in peoples' eyes when they realise that they have made something special. Groups realising their individual ideas. My greatest challenge is to make a difference in a short time, perhaps through challenging other people's perceptions.

What hopes do you have for the people you work with?

That they may see and look at images in a different way as a result of being in a workshop – be more critical. That they will pick up a camera and have a go themselves. That they see how to use the 'tricks of the trade'. That they get a buzz from what they are doing, even if it is simply seeing something slightly differently than they did before.

How do the people you work with affect your work?

Adults with learning disabilities are open and receptive to ideas if allowed the chance. Each group I work with completely defines how I run that session. I have to be prepared to change my plans completely on the spot. It is a two-way process. Individuals give me ideas on how to communicate and hopefully I encourage them. It is important that my groups enjoy themselves.

Do you work with other educators outside your immediate workplace?

I don't have an immediate workplace. I work in different places every day, so yes I do work with others. I work with my partner sometimes, helping each other on our own projects and sometimes inventing new projects.

Can you describe the contexts in which you work?

I often work with people who have never done this kind of work before. The experience I offer is outside what they would normally do. We often have to make do with very limited resources but I see this as a stepping stone. I continually use the historical context of the origin of film in my sessions. This is where I start. I work in many different environments – primary schools, secondary schools, adult education centres, day centres, neighbourhood centres, film theatres and museums.

How do these contexts affect the way you work?

I think I like to break down previous barriers and expectations and provide a fresh start. Working in a wide range of environments is a good way of doing this and helps keep my own ideas developing.

What are your hopes for the future?

They change all the time and depend on what I am doing at the moment. I would like to carry on gaining experience and getting better at what I do now and see where that leads me. I don't think about the future very much.

Helen

Who are you?

I am a partner, mum, teacher, friend, daughter, devisor of children's plays, a team worker, and an enthusiast about contemporary theatre.

Why did you choose to be this?

I partly always thought I would — a sense of destiny fulfilled. Partly wasn't sure what else my abilities and interests qualified me to do.

What has influenced you to take this direction in life?

Two or three teachers who inspired me in very different ways. They all broke the mould in terms of my experience in school. Later, I found a job in a school which was trying to offer a better alternative to disadvantaged kids. I still have a desire to be a thinking professional, this desire being fulfilled recently by working with teachers who have been influential to me as an adult.

What were the most meaningful parts of your education?

I have vivid memories of key lessons during my time at secondary school, often linked to theatre trips. The final year of my English degree was an important time, as was my teaching course. More recently I had a sabbatical year with a team of teachers from a small school working on whole school development. Most importantly, working with kids continues to educate me.

In way ways does education fit in with values held at home?

It was always seen as important in that without exams you didn't get a job, but not so important that you should over-reach yourself as a girl (these messages came mainly from my mum). My dad had hopes of me rising through the ranks as he had, with or without higher education. He had a real desire for me to be successful in the public sense of the word.

Why do you continue to be involved in education?

I get a real buzz when interacting/learning with and from kids and colleagues. It feels like it matters to a whole lot of young people and adults – I can't understand when it doesn't matter to other people. I feel remotivated after suffering a period of burn-out. I have reinvented myself, and am as enthusiastic now as when I first started teaching 18 years ago.

What are your strengths?

Enthusiasm – I can inspire and influence others. Ideas and relationships with young people. I wish I could be better organised and prepared.

What influences you now?

My family, all the kids I work with, reading, an involvement in politics of education. I am still driven by a sense of inequality that faces many kids as they grow up. Colleagues who share a sense of education as the key for us all.

What are the biggest challenges you face?

My lack of energy, a continuous lack of resources, the many government changes, teachers who hate kids, the National Curriculum. I am often frustrated with my lack of ambition for traditional career ladder climbing. I need the energy for being creative and ambitious in terms of my own personal teaching projects.

What are your greatest joys?

Having my ideas recognised as valuable by others. We couldn't produce what we do without each other.

What are your hopes for those you work with?

That they become more creative, less status- and money-orientated and less image-conscious. Most of all that they enjoy it.

Who do you work with?

Some of the people I work with are creative team workers who are in the same position as me, often feeling powerless. I think I create opportunities to share power in school with the kids. Others are under-valued colleagues and outside agencies. The kids are struggling, bright, but unsure of their direction. A bit like me. It often feels as though I work with mostly underprivileged kids and over-privileged adults. Some of us are working towards more democracy in the workplace, but most adults try to keep the politics out of a workplace heaving with institutionalised politics of destruction.

There is a pressure on the kids to conform to middle-class attitudes and this leads to an unhealthy atmosphere. This insecurity and lack of self-worth leads to a volatile community, charged with excitement, some fear, and much untapped talent.

What are your hopes for the future?

I would love to be involved in a school created by a team of inspirational, hard-working people with a vision of students as interesting individuals. I know so many gifted teachers. I feel that between us we could create a fabulous environment if funding was available. My other dream is to open an Arts Centre attached to a school for young people to experiment with their creativity.

Reflections

We began these interviews by asking each other 'Who are you?' over and over. This helped us reveal where we were starting from both as teachers and as writers. Sometimes it was a name, sometimes a profession or sometimes a relationship with which we first identified ourselves. By repeating the question we uncovered, often to our amazement, just how many things we are, how many 'hats' we wear.

Looking over the interviews it is obvious that each writer's background both as a child and as an adult has been a key influence on their becoming educators. However, within these stories there is a range of expectation – from knowledge being the 'key' and learning a lifelong process, through to 'do well ... but not *too* well'. The challenge for us as teachers is to support this multiplicity of expectations brought into school by pupils and their parents and carers. How will we respond to the various levels of support, pressure or *apparent* disinterest that each parent will bring when we meet or communicate with them?

The variety of styles in the responses is also striking. Even within a group of what might be called 'like-minded people' there is a massive range of experience. This 'like-mindedness' comes through most strongly when we talk about our strengths as educators. It also becomes clear that many of us 'fell into' our present careers, rather than having had a clear vision or understanding about what our strengths were. What was it that delayed this understanding until so late in our lives? Is this delay necessarily a good or a bad thing? Why weren't this group of writers success-fully 'squared off' and pigeonholed into future careers? The people who have sup-ported the writers' growing realisation of what they might become, now seem to be the biggest influence on their lives and interestingly many of these people were not trained teachers.

It is also striking how many of the writers see teaching as a part of their own continued development, as well as being concerned to develop the students they teach. Again, the variety of responses about our futures – from 'I don't think about it much' to a definite list of aims – is another indication that there is no such thing as a fixed mould for becoming a teacher.

Questions for your journal

We would like you to follow the same process as the authors in researching your personal starting point. After asking the question 'Who are you" over and over we had to allow for long silences in order to make sure we could dredge up all the dif-ferent roles we play in and out of our roles as educators. Our responses to this ques-tion form the opening of each of our statements. You might want to try this same activity – it would make the perfect opening to your journal. So, as many times as you can, answer this question.

Who are you? Who are you? Who are you? Who are you? Who are you? Who are you?

Follow this up by writing about your most vivid memory of your own schooling. Try to remember it in as much detail as possible. If you feel confident enough, share it with a friend or colleague. Get them to ask you questions about your 'memory'. This often helps you remember things you thought you had forgotten.

The list that follows is adapted from the questions we worked with to come up with our personal statements. Try to answer this as honestly as possible to form the next section of your journal.

• Why do you think you want to be a teacher?

- What has influenced you to take this direction in your life?
- What were the most meaningful parts of your own education (not just in formal schooling)?
- In what ways does education fit in with values held at home?
- What do you think your strengths will be as an educator?
- How do you think you will need to change to become a good teacher?
- What/who influences you most now?
- What are the biggest challenges that you face? The biggest frustrations? The greatest joys and satisfactions?
- What hopes do you have for the people you work with?
- Do you have an image of the people with whom you want to work?
- What are the main experiences you would like a learner in your class to have?
- What are your hopes for the future?

Share your responses with someone you feel comfortable talking to. Question each other and use these questions to expand your initial journal entries. Finally, think back over what you have read in this chapter. Try to answer these questions; again enter your thoughts in your journal.

- Which author do you remember most about?
- Why do you think this is?
- Which statement did you agree most strongly with? Why do you think you have chosen this statement?
- Which statement did you disagree most strongly with? Why do you think you have chosen this statement?

Part 2

OUR EXPERIENCES OF EDUCATION

Overview

Teachers often complain that everyone they meet or listen to feels they are an expert on education. Many people from outside the profession all seem to feel qualified to offer an opinion. Of course, we only notice this when we feel unfairly criticised. In many ways everyone is an expert. We all attended school. Different schools, of course, but often our experiences were very similar. Despite this, our experiences are very personal. We all have a personal knowledge of schools and ideas about schooling which we have developed during this time. We have visions of the way we would have liked things to be, visions for how we would like schools to be in the future.

Perhaps more importantly our own identities are tied up in experiences we had in school. And our image of ourselves during our time in school will affect the type of teacher we want to become. If we want to be effective teachers we cannot simply react to everyday events in the moment and make on-the-spot decisions. We need to be able to respond flexibly and quickly but in a way which fits a well thought through process and set of values. If we think carefully about how we reacted to our own time in school, and why, we can start to see the sort of teacher we want to be. Most importantly, we can become aware of ourselves developing as teachers. We begin to act with an awareness of ourselves and so feel more in control. We are not simply always thinking on our feet, making it up as we go along.

By remembering the way we acted in particular social situations we can see ourselves as contributing to the way things were, and how the way we acted at the time affected the way particular events developed. We can see either how we were powerful in that situation or analyse what made us powerless. This can help us see ourselves as individuals capable of making a difference.

In order to change from being a learner in school to being a teacher, several things must happen. We learn that there is more to teaching than simply passing on knowledge. We learn that relationships with our pupils are the most important thing, and that relationships are very personal and individual things. We can only move to form positive relationships with our pupils by thinking how our teachers formed positive relationships with us, or the blocks that they put in the way of our learning. As a teacher we become the person responsible for creating a 'positive learning environment'. This phrase often crops up and prospective teachers ask 'How can we create a positive learning environment?' It is frustrating to be told that there is no simple answer. But we have all sat in such 'positive learning environments', or in environ-

ments which clearly were not conducive to learning. By analysing what made these classrooms successes and failures, from our own point of view, we can see the possibilities open to us as teachers.

Anecdoting

The process we followed in order to write this section was not simply a telling of stories, although this formed a part of each session. Rather, we used a process which has been called 'anecdoting'. This is a focused discussion which allows individuals to actively reconstruct their experiences, often through questioning from others in the group. The hope is that it will allow participants to draw common threads and generalisations from these experiences. They can begin to see the connections and draw out what is important in the stories.

This is done by all the group focusing on a single issue – perhaps a single memory from primary school – they then write about this memory and share it with the group. One of the group then reads their anecdote, others in the group react to the anecdote by adding in memories of their own which are triggered at this point. When this is exhausted, another member of the group shares their anecdote and the process is repeated. At the end of the session the group as a whole decides what the important issues are which have been raised by the discussions. We selected memories which we wanted to share with a wider readership. You may wish to explore anecdoting with friends or colleagues to discover what issues and experiences are most important to you.

Chapter 2

Our Best Teachers

Introduction

A sum. Six years in primary school equals at least six teachers (many more now because of specialist teachers in primary schools). Five years in secondary school multiplied by ten subjects multiplied by the number of teachers who left during a year multiplied by the number of times you changed schools. Add on your driving instructor, your tap dance teacher and your piano teacher. If you do the sum you may well find out that you have had the best (and worst) part of 100 teachers.

It was surprising when we sat down to discuss this chapter to find that some of us did not have favourite teachers. To those of us who did this seems extraordinarily sad, because we can think of many individual teachers who gave us skills and understanding which we use daily, 30 or more years later. Our discussions definitely revealed some how-not-to's, but what follows are predominantly positive influences. These are teachers we knew as 'real' people, the ones who knew us best. We will all, at one time or another, be someone's favourite, and someone's least favourite, teacher; that is a fact of life. The following anecdotes show, however, that knowing our students well is the key to making a true connection with them, and creating environments in which real learning can take place.

Marc

Mr Jones, an English teacher, was my favourite teacher but I can't really explain why. He taught me when I was 13 years old, over 30 years ago, in the year he retired. My clearest memory of him is an occasion when he inadvertently provided me with one of the footsteps into adulthood a year after his retirement, when he returned to school for a visit. Seeing him from a distance, I watched him approach and greeted him with a hearty, 'Hello, Sir'. He quite clearly didn't have the faintest idea who I was, and smiling, passed by without breaking his stride. I liked him enough not to mind, and realised that just because I thought *he* was important, he was under no obligation to pay me the slightest bit of attention, ever.

Why was he my favourite teacher? I wondered about this long before we started thinking about the question as a group. Although I can still remember where I sat in his lessons, which room they were in and other details, there is no trace left of how he taught or any specific lesson that he taught. I remember quiet lessons. I am sure he had a lovely speaking voice, but I can't remember that either. I think perhaps he was one of those people who are able to appear to give you their full attention even when they are thinking about something else. I estimate he must have stopped teaching in 1965 and wonder at the change within and outside education he must have seen during his life.

Alec Bruce also retired the year after he taught me. I loathed chemistry at school but was edging towards a real interest in it as a mature student when I had to attend Alec's lectures as a part of my degree. He ensured I was hooked. I have used his talk on safety as a model for many such talks I have had to give over the years. I have not dared to have *quite* so many explosions as he did, but I hope to instil the focus he did. Just before shutting my eyes I saw the whole of the front row of the lecture theatre ducking below their desks in anticipation of the ball of flame which they knew must be the outcome of the series of staged mishaps Alec had relentlessly unfolded just a few feet from our unprotected heads. I know why I liked Alec. He could make the driest bits of chemistry funny and relevant. He treated his audience as adults, and woe betide anyone who was childishly late. You felt as if you would be taken to an understanding of any topic, if you just gave him your fill attention. He commanded that attention.

James

Rather than a best teacher I remember a best lesson, or series of English lessons. I was about 15 at the time and we were studying *Macbeth*. I was very bored with the lesson and with the text; I was not inspired by the play although I remember enjoying the poetry. The teacher seemed to sense the class boredom and tried introducing the play in several different ways. The class still did not respond. The next day when we came back to the class, he picked a section from the play, the appearance of Banquo's ghost, and got us to act it out. He complimented us and then started to tell us about his time working for Idi Amin and compared the situation in Uganda with the stories and themes in the play. These stories were vivid enough to hold our attention and to provoke discussion over the political issues which were raised. The teacher had managed to open me up to Shakespeare and to politics in one brief moment. I remember the discussion becoming quite animated and going on for some time. In order to focus us back on the play he pronounced, 'Anyway, we'd better stop there. It is getting too political and I might get into trouble for talking politics with you'. Often, in future lessons, he would open up similar discussions when he sensed a lull in our attention, always ending the discussions in the same way, 'Well, we are getting political now.' We would return to our work, refreshed from having our say.

Debbion

Marie Williams, my history teacher. She's an Irish Catholic who makes her own clothes, and teaches at an all girls school where she is also headteacher. She is about ten years older than me. She had an ability to make us all feel important, so although I thought she was my friend, everyone in the class did too. I hated history but liked her, so I paid particular attention. She *is* my friend now and she has a way of ringing me when something is wrong.

She is a cockney who uses long words and made me realise that working-class people can be as academic and intelligent as anyone else. I remember her being proud of me when I was at school and never doubting me. Once when I was in the upper sixth I was working at home and she rang me. She said, 'The thing is, darlin', if you're able to do it on your own, they (the teachers) will feel redundant and they won't 'ave it so get in 'ere now.' She always told it like it was so that I could make informed choices from a very early age about what I wanted to do and how best to go about it.

Another important teacher was my best friend's mum. She was not my school teacher but she was a teacher and I spent a lot of time round her house. I used to pull the curtains back and dance and choreograph things in the reflection. She was so supportive of what I wanted to do and her encouragement helped me develop a positive identity.

Helen

My best teacher was born and brought up in Marple, near Glossop – my home town. This immediate and close connection was very important to me. She taught me when I attended a school in the south-eastern commuter belt. Her dad ran the sweet shop next to the railway arches in Glossop and I remember going in the shop one day and being disappointed that he wasn't as excited as I was about the coincidence. She was half romantic, opaque and dreamy, and half *Woman's Own*. She always had a copy sticking out of her packed school bag. She had long thin fingers with which she smoothed open the book while asking you gently what exactly had made you notice that interesting thing about *Julius Caesar* or *The Merchant of Venice*. She talked with an accent which was home for me but stood out for everyone else in this Sussex classroom. One of my most vivid memories of her is the day she took us into the school hall to act out a passage from Shakespeare. We were so unused to anything other than sitting in alphabetical order in desks in rows that we reacted with wild enthusiasm to our new-found freedom. The Head of Department, the one with the frizz of hair flopping over wildly staring eyes, descended from her room to tell us all to behave ourselves and do as we were told. We took notice and were good next lesson but I thought no less of her for having been admonished by her Head of Department. I did not see this as a weakness. Rather, I valued her for the risks she took with us. She laughed with us, read everything we wrote, loved her subject, never shouted … lived with a radical intellectual and, sadly, died young.

Jasbir

I was one of the members of the group who couldn't think of a particular teacher who had made an impact on me. Yet so many had in different ways. Perhaps my memory was clouded because of the constant differences between home and school. My energy was taken up in learning how to function in those two very different environments.

My father had come to this country in the early 1950s expecting to stay a few years and then return to the Panjab having earned some money, to set up a new home. My mother joined my father in the late 1950s and I was born in Bradford. Throughout my early life and early schooling I was conscious that we would be returning 'home' fairly soon – where this 'home' was I was not clear. At school I learnt to fit in and become accepted – in a way I can see that I have spent the rest of my life trying to 'fit in'.

I believe that one of the things that makes a good teacher is that they allow individuals to take control of their own learning. perhaps I never really felt in control which is why I don't feel that I ever had a 'best' teacher. I always seemed to be trying to please others – my family, my teachers – yet, despite this, I enjoyed school, I wanted to learn. I loved sports, science and maths. More than anything else I adored double hockey on a Monday morning after break. First lesson was maths and I would get myself a seat by the window so I could keep an eye on the weather, praying it would not rain.

Hockey was wonderful. Here I did feel in control, and for once it seemed everyone wanted to be on my side. I was chosen for the school team but then my problems began as the two worlds of home and school collided. We were expected to make our own way to away matches on a Saturday morning. To my mother, the thought of a teenage girl wandering around town was unacceptable and there was no one in my family who could take me to the way matches. I was not sure what to do.

Independence seemed to be encouraged by my friends' parents, yet in my culture certain kinds of independence were frowned on. I also did not want my friends to see me constantly being supervised.

So I only played in home matches. My PE teacher could not understand why someone so conscientious would let them down so often, and I could not explain. There seemed to be no middle ground. Was it my job to explain to the teachers or the school's role to find out why I would only play in half the matches? It seemed that the pressures of being the only pupil from a different background were for me far greater than being part of a group.

Perhaps my teachers were well meaning but simply did not take the time to understand. For instance, I cannot remember in my primary years ever admitting I could speak Panjabi; I was actually embarrassed about it. When I was about ten years old I can remember a French girl coming into the class. We all had to learn to say 'Bonjour, comment ça-va', so that she would feel welcome. I thought this was a great idea but wondered why the teachers didn't do this for any of the Asian pupils who joined the school with little or no English.

So, although I have no individual memories of influential 'good teachers', I do carry with me experiences which have influenced the way I work in schools as a teacher and headteacher. I feel very strongly that we must value and build on a childs' experiences at home. Teachers need to know the whole child, perhaps through such things as home visits before the child starts school, certainly through talking with their pupils. I am aware that children often arrive at school bright, bouncy, full of curiosity, ready to learn – and that if we are not careful we can destroy these qualities.

Vicky

Thinking about this has made me delve into corners of my mind, labelled 'school', which I usually choose not to enter. Three teachers spring to mind who I knew at different stages of my school years, all of whom it would be fun to see again if I had the chance. I have decided to compare them to see if I can discover what it is I liked about them and if there are any similarities. They did not teach the subjects I was 'best' in, or even my favourite subjects by any means.

I knew Mrs Toplis for a long time as she taught me at primary school and again in the last two years of my secondary school. The main thing I can remember about her are her wiry, masculine features which seemed to fit her eccentric personality. She always wore trousers (except once in the summer when she appeared in a cotton frock in an assembly, much to our amazement) and rode a bike to school. She brought history alive by explaining it in complicated boxes, all interlinked and differently coloured, using very serious chalky writing on the blackboard. I remember being impressed by this. Most of the class did not pass history O level and I remember thinking at the time that I loved her lessons, but for some reason the history bits did not seem to stick in my mind at all. I remember her saying that the worst thing anyone could say was that they were bored, and never to read a book without a pencil. In other words, take notice of the ideas and notes that you make in our head.

When she left, there was a leaving party at her house where she had dug her own 3′ by 4′ swimming pool to tread water in. We discovered that the room she slept in was tiny and completely lined with books. The bed seemed to hover somewhere above the top shelf. Mrs Toplis retired the same year I left school and said she was going to canoe round the world – I hope she did.

I did not know Mrs Tear for very long but I think she was the first 'modern' teacher I had. She was our dance/drama teacher. She was young and we worked on projects we could relate to. One summer 'do' seemed to involve prancing around in a circle to Pink Floyd in torn trousers and skirts we had sprayed silver and hung on fences to dry around the school. She introduced me to sound effects records, we listened to water bubbling through headphones, and I loved it.

The third teacher I think of when I remember teachers I liked is Mrs Jones who demystified Shakespeare for me, translating it with inspiration. I remember it taking a long time to understand and come to like the plays we studied, but when I finally did it was thrilling and I scribbled for hours at home. She showed me how to read a story to make it come alive. I particularly remember her sitting on the edge of a desk correcting someone on the use of the word 'lady'. 'for instance', she said, 'I am not a lady, it does not describe me, but I am a woman.' She was a strong woman with a sense of purpose. It was Mrs Jones who suggested to me at a break time just before I left school, in an offhand, but in retrospect, perhaps an astute way, that I should remain in education for a bit longer. 'Oh, go on,' she said. I did!

These three teachers were all independent women who presented themselves as real, open people, with lives outside school. I felt that they wanted to be there, teaching me, and that they had a will to communicate passionately about their work. I felt that they cared about me and that they liked me. They all seemed in charge of their classes and commanded our attention.

Dorothy

"I do not remember any good teachers during my time in school. What I do remember is an individual who taught me the best lesson I ever learnt soon after leaving school. Let me set the scene.

Six months after leaving school and still out of work, I signed up on the Youth Opportunities Programme (YOP) and was placed at a local estate agents. On my arrival the manager told me that I was the fourth YOP trainee they had had. The last young person who had left only a week previously had been punctual, polite, efficient, a real paragon of virtue. 'Why didn't you keep her, then?' I asked. He looked at me as if I was deranged and replied, 'Don't be silly – she was only a YOP trainee. Why buy a cow when you can get the milk for free?' This exchange completely demoralised me as I knew that no matter how hard I worked I would never be offered employment. The owner of the business simply saw me as cheap labour; my main duties were to run errands, make coffee and take photocopies, I was not taught anything about the business and worked almost entirely in isolation. I could not leave otherwise my benefit would be withdrawn, which I could not afford as I was only 17, living away from home and needed to pay my rent and buy food.

However, a loophole existed. If I was dismissed from my placement my social security payments would not be penalised. So I worked hard at being late, being rude and inefficient and was soon, thankfully, sacked. This happened on a Friday afternoon. I emptied my desk of my few belongings and wandered miserably into the city centre. I was happy to leave the awful estate agents but worried about what the future might hold. I happened to bump into a community worker I knew called Ricky Stennett; he asked me what I was doing and why. I told him and the three-hour conversation that followed changed my life.

He was curious to know why, if I had six O levels, had I never considered A levels. I laughed and said, 'Don't be silly – people like me don't do A levels.'

He questioned me further. 'They just don't,' I said. He looked horrified and asked me to come for a coffee so that he could talk to me. He then spent the next three hours persuading me that people 'like me' did and could do A levels and that, if I wanted to, I could do some and them move on to a degree.

I was incredulous, sceptical and doubting. It may seem odd that I had never considered myself to be A level material, but that was the case. I had never been told before that I could do A levels; no one at school or elsewhere had ever mentioned this as a possibility. An elite band of 16 pupils from my year group at comprehensive school had been selected to move on to A levels; the rest of us were encouraged to leave and find work, or perhaps undertake a vocational qualification at the local further education college. It never occurred to me that further study was a viable option.

So when I got up on this Friday in 1978 my future held no vision of further education; by the end of the day it did. Ricky Stennett spent the whole of the afternoon, over rapidly cooling and almost untouched coffee, reinforcing my mother's message that I could be whatever I wanted to be, but he took it a step further. He believed in me. He had no need to give up a precious afternoon in a crowded schedule to persuade a 17-year-old that she could go further, but he did. By the end of the afternoon he had persuaded me to enrol at the local FE college on the following Monday morning. I did, and three A levels, an honours degree, a professional postgraduate qualification and a diploma in Teaching English as a Foreign Language later, the rest is history.

Ricky Stennett was my best teacher because he believed in me. He made me realise that although I thought I had set my goals high, they were in fact quite low. My goals were influenced by the beliefs and expectations of others and I had not learnt to look outside of these. By believing in me he taught me to believe in myself.

This is the best lesson I have ever learnt. It has also become the best lesson I teach and has influenced the way I have worked with others from my very first teaching session until now. I feel that lack of confidence and self belief affects the ability to learn and that believing in yourself and having others believe in you is a necessity in the learning process. Simply having someone telling you that you can achieve whatever you are striving for is an important part of making that learning possible. This seems to me to be much more important than this thing often called 'intelligence' when it comes to learning and succeeding. Many 'intelligent' people fail because they are expected to fail, or are told they will fail due to some social factor – they are Black, they are female, they live on a council estate, and so on. Good teachers put these prejudices aside and focus on what the child can do, rather than what they cannot.

Tony

I felt somewhat left out of the discussions about best and favourite teachers as I am afraid I have few fond memories of my teachers, certainly no one I would confer the label of 'best' on. However, as the conversation progressed I realised who my best teacher *is*. He is my piano teacher. Yes, at the age of 38 I have taken up piano lessons again. It is a fascinating process to be a beginner and to reflect on how the way we work in classrooms can affect the way pupils come to see our subject and us as teachers.

During my first lesson my teacher was very dismissive of the value of exams: he wanted me to enjoy the piano for its own sake. He was surprised at my request to sit exams as he did not see this as a true judge of our success. I was unconvinced at first as I did not know how else I could measure his and my effectiveness. During the first lesson he also changed the fingering on a piece of music I thought I had mastered. He explained that the fingering I was using made the piece sound clumsy; I was playing the correct notes but 'music is much more than just the right notes'. Of course, when I came to play him the piece using the new fingering I couldn't make my fingers obey my brain and so the notes fell out in a jumble. I felt useless. I wanted to practise one hand at a time and then put hands together when I felt confident; he was firm in the view that I should *never* practise one hand at a time. I argued that I had been taught by this method in the past, but he remained unimpressed. He explained to me that he saw one of his roles as providing the motivation to practise so I wouldn't appear foolish during lessons. I left this first lesson rather confused, but several weeks later, the piece sounds much better with the new fingering and I am more comfortable playing it. I no longer want to do exams. I trust my teacher's judgement about the level we are playing at, and I practise, not so much to avoid looking foolish, but because I would feel that I have let my teacher down if I don't. I also practise because I am very much enjoying playing.

One lesson had a particular effect on my relationship with the teacher and myself as a learner. My lesson had changed days and I arrived slightly early. I sat in the corner of the room and was relieved to find another adult being taught. I was not on my own. At the very end of the lesson my teacher took over the piano to play the piece my colleague was struggling on. It was beautiful – I could feel my confidence in the teacher growing; I wanted to be able to play like that, I wanted him to show me how. I sat and worked out how many piano lessons I would be able to have in the rest of my life and convinced myself I had enough time to get to play like that. During the lesson he commented to me that he enjoyed teaching adults as they had a musicality that young children did not have, a more mature appreciation of music; I don't know if this is true but it sounded plausible and made me feel good. The same day he gave me a new book. He let me sight-read a piece and then went back to his cupboard to get out the next book in the series. He told me that if I could sight-read that piece

I could immediately move up a book. I left the lesson with my new book under my arm and a skip in my step. Literally.

More recently, in fact the week before our final meeting to write this book, I had my best lesson so far. I am still trying to work out how I can recreate the feeling I got from the lesson for learners in my classrooms. The lesson went on as usual, I played a piece through as if in performance, being rewarded by a tick and a new piece to work at. (Yes, even 38-year-olds like ticks in three books.) We then worked at the other two pieces I am learning. With about five minutes to go my teacher asked me to sight-read my new piece. I managed to play it through haltingly but reasonably accurately. I was pleased and so, I felt, was my teacher. At this point he said, 'Have we ever played a duet?' We never have – I wondered why he thought we may have done. 'Let's have a go,' he said and we moved over to his grand piano. I couldn't believe I was going to have a go on this beautiful instrument. He put a piece of music in front of me, said, 'It starts on E,' and off he went. I suddenly found myself playing along, hardly having time to think, but it felt like I was actually playing music. For the first time I felt like a piano player rather than someone learning to play the piano. We played the piece through four times. I realised I was sight-reading, feeling for notes without looking down, listening for pitch and tone, all of those things I had been working at for so long, but I was doing them almost without thinking. It was one of the most exciting five minutes for a long time.

Reflection

So, those of us who had favourite teachers in school, remember those who we had confidence in and who were in command of their class and pupils. They all seemed to genuinely like and care about the subject they were teaching, whether it was chemistry in university or playing the piano with adults.

For four of us it is an English teacher who we have made space for in our memories. Is this a coincidence? Did they help us develop the way that we think more than teachers of other subjects? Is the demystifying of Shakespeare such a revelation? Or is it that this helps us to wake up to language, to communication? Perhaps it is one of the first steps to being made to think more deeply, or maybe the first time we were talked to by an adult in a philosophical way?

There are other important similarities between the teachers we have chosen. All have human qualities, they made us feel good about ourselves, they made us see things are possible and they justified our existence as unique human beings, not simply faceless pupils. These teachers made us feel as though we had an important voice in their classrooms. Helen, Vicky and Debbion found positive role models in strong women who did not mystify or play down the importance of their lives outside school. How different this is to the image many pupils have of teachers as existing purely between the hours of 8.30 a.m. and 3.00 p.m.

It seems that the best teachers know their students well. For Jasbir in particular the fact that none of her teachers took the time to get to know her led to a feeling of isolation in school. It is much easier to communicate with someone if you understand them. Teachers have to communicate not just knowledge, ideas and skills, but also be persuasive about the importance of education, the need to work with others. Occasionally teachers have to persuade a student that something they have done is unacceptable, and then prepare them for not doing it again. They have to be prepared to be unpopular. Sometimes *very* unpopular; the key is being prepared for it.

What makes a teacher popular? Some are chummier than their colleagues and make a big show of this. When you become a teacher you will have to make your judgements about these people. Are they looking for approval or the respect of real friends? Some teachers seem to be almost universally unpopular; are they simply stricter, or do they fail to relate to their students? Strictness or classroom discipline, is often an issue with pupils. However, balancing this with the sorts of risks Helen describes her favourite teacher taking is important. This can be difficult for a teacher short on confidence, or one who has not thought the issue through. Put simply, the student whose work is being disrupted will think you are a very good teacher if you can create an environment within the classroom in which they can work without interruption. However, you will not be thanked if you create places in which uninterrupted work is possible, but the activities you offer are dry and unexciting.

Those who did not have favourite teachers look back on their schooling with a realisation of the influence it has had on them, but also with unanswered questions. Why did no teacher ever really connect with me? Why did adults outside school have to be the ones to encourage me or believe in myself? How can teachers recognise the fact that many of the children are bilingual and even multilingual? Why do teachers seem to be more comfortable introducing 'modern' foreign languages from Europe rather than the community languages which are spoken in the streets outside the school? Jasbir wonders why it was that she felt the need to hide her linguistic skills in order to 'fit' in, in her primary classrooms. The best teachers here are those strong enough to challenge institutional prejudices, although Dorothy had to wait until she had left formal education to find a 'teacher' who would offer her the belief she desired and needed to continue in education.

It seems that the challenge is to know the child so that, as a teacher, we know what they will value sharing and what they may want to remain secret. Perhaps that is what is shared by those who cannot remember a favourite or best teacher – they cannot remember anyone taking the time to get to know them.

Questions for your journal

Many of us have model teachers in our minds. The idea for this section of your journal is that you can be explicit for yourself about what it is that you value in those who have taught you. Which of their characteristics do you want to adapt and make your own? This section of your journal can also help you define for yourself the image you want to put across to those you work with. So, new page, sharpen the pencil and:

- Which of the teachers described in this chapter do you wish you had had?
- Why do you think you have made this choice?
- Who was your favourite teacher in school?
- Why have you chosen this teacher over all the others? What was special about them?
- List the things you think make a good teacher.
- Which of these qualities do you think you have?
- How can you gain the qualities you think you are missing?

Chapter 3

Why do they think we will ever forget?

Introduction

This book for the most part focuses on the positive force that is education. However, we mustn't forget that some people's memories of school are filled with feelings of fear and humiliation. These negative feelings can remain with us for our whole lives and can be disempowering as we feel alienated from what were supposed to be the 'best days of our lives'. These feelings can remain with us, having been passed from parents to their children, making all contact with school difficult on all sides.

Some teachers seem to bring with them a regime of ruling by fear. They almost become lost in their own power base. Their areas of the school are motivated by punishment: the art teacher who used to poke you with a set square, the science teacher who would hit you with Bunsen burner tubing. Their pupils remember little of the art or science they were supposed to be teaching.

So we offer the following anecdotes as reminders that there may be teachers whose ways of working make you feel very uncomfortable. You will also work with pupils who expect to be controlled through bullying, either because that is what they are used to outside school or because they have become used to it in their earlier experience of school. You will need to find your own ways to challenge such unacceptable practices, and ways of supporting pupils who on occasions are bullied by teachers. Yes, such teachers do still exist. There are not very many of them, thankfully, but we have all come across them during our recent time in schools. These teachers serve as a reminder of the importance of offering ourselves as positive role models – teachers who can offer children positive memories both of schooling and of learning and perhaps, most importantly, of themselves.

Helen

❝I am sitting in a mixed class of 9–11-year-olds, a lot of kids, all sitting in rows facing the teacher and the blackboard. The teacher is Miss Emy, the head mistress, definitely a head*mistress*, an ageing spinster, with a booming voice, 'You great big BOOBY!' her favourite term of abuse. In this class the expectation was that the top five or ten pupils would pass the 11+, but the whole of the rest of the class seemed to be taught nothing but 'how to pass the 11+' too.

Earlier in the week we had been tested on words which sound the same. Miss Emy would say the word, put it in a sentence and we would write the correct spelling of the word. Questions 1–20 (why are there always 20 questions?) every Friday (why always on a Friday?). However, we had now reached the afternoon, the time I loved, the time to be creative and I was lost in story-writing, so absorbed that all other distractions disappeared. Suddenly, I felt like a car running out of petrol. I looked at my book in which I had written 'I didn't no ...' and I felt my concentration snap out of creative mode. There was something wrong, I'd better check.

We were not encouraged to ask a friend. It was cheating, we were told. We shouldn't talk in class except to the teacher. We were told. They would probably get it wrong as well. We were told. I went to the dictionary, but that couldn't sort out my problem. I'd better ask Miss Emy.

Join the queue – wait my turn – don't fidget in the queue.

'Yes, Helen.' I'll show Miss Emy my book – I'm not sure I know how to explain.

'Miss Emy, I don't know how to spell 'no' in this ...'

'I BEG YOUR PARDON?'

That tone, the rumble before the eruption, how could I stop it? I blush, stumble for words, stutter, 'Er, ... I ... d .. d ... don't ... know how to ... sp ... sp ... spell ... no.'

She shouts, 'EVERYBODY, put your pens down ... NOW. This girl (sneer) doesn't know how to spell (pause for dramatic effect) NO (total disbelief).'

Titters from the class, more blushing from me, a voice in my mind explaining to them all that they didn't understand, that it was because I *knew* there were two ways, and wasn't sure which I needed in this sentence, and if they would just look at my work they'd see why it wasn't such a stupid question.

'YOU GREAT BIG BOOBY!. N O spells no! Now get on with your work. ... Everyone.'

I sit back down – finish my story. Miss Emy's comment on my afternoon of work was 7/10, poor ending – learn your spellings!

James

Many of my memories of school and teachers consist of a daily ritual of humiliation of students by their teachers. This ritual humiliation is epitomised by a teacher who had a habit of writing things that people said aloud in class on the board. This quote would be followed by the initials of the child who had spoken. One lad, an Irish lad, was called Vincent Dougherty. As the teacher initialled his comments with VD, she looked around the class for the cheap laugh, knowing she could not be exposed as a bully as she could claim she had done no wrong.

English lessons during my first year at grammar school seemed to consist entirely of reading aloud. I remember the fear as you sat hoping not to be picked. But the time would draw nearer as the teacher relentlessly went around the class picking child after child. You would try to read ahead, guessing the section you may be asked to read, searching for words you didn't know. The fear was increased by the teacher constantly attempting to catch people out by demanding faster response and understanding. As I think back I can hear her knocking some of the kids' pronunciations which she considered wrong, either due to a slowness in reading aloud or because of their accents. The pupils she humiliated in this way were all either working class, or had an accent different to her norm.

In contrast she would often focus on her favourite pupils, being effusive in her congratulations if she was pleased with their contribution. As they year went by she became more pointedly vindictive to individuals. I remember one lad pronouncing lieutenant in the American style (loo-tenant); no doubt this is what he had heard in films and on television. The teacher did not correct him, simply asked him to pronounce it again. In a rising panic my colleague simply repeated 'loo-tenant' again and again, unaware of the expected pronunciation (left-tenant). Similarly, another friend often mispronounced 'interpreted' as 'interpretated'. I am afraid the teacher's fixation with this means that I often make the same mistake today. This is the teacher I remembered most clearly when we first began talking about schools. I have an image of myself standing at her desk. She holds a rolled-up newspaper in her hand and asks me what she is holding. I tell her, 'A newspaper, Miss.' I pronounce it 'noospaper'. She hits me with the rolled-up paper and asks me again. The scene is repeated as I have no idea what I am doing wrong in her eyes. To this day I cannot remember how this charade ended. Unfortunately, I only have these memories of her lessons. I cannot remember any of the books we worked on with her, or the content of any of her lessons, just memories of fear and panic.

In contrast, a different English teacher in the same school once singled out a Scottish classmate and allowed him an unusually extended session of reading out loud. At first he allowed the titters and giggles and then interrupted the reading mid-flow to explain that the reason he was allowing Iain to continue was because his thick Edinburgh brogue was 'pleasing to the ear'. He then pulled apart words phonetically to illustrate how Iain's accent was actually closer to Shakespearean language than our own accents. Seeing Iain in a favourable academic light meant we all had to reassess our view of him.

Jasbir

It was May Day and our teacher, Mrs Green, had told us all about the celebration including May Pole dancing and choosing the May Queen and her attendants. This was going to be a big event; parents would be coming to watch. The local paper was going to send a photographer so we may get our pictures in the newspaper. There was a lot of hard work required from all of us to ensure that the performance would be as professional as possible. The May Queen and her acolytes would obviously be the 'stars' in this performance and we all became very excited over who would be chosen.

I was sitting in the second row and felt very close to the teacher. She was about to select the May Queen and her attendants. She had already said she was looking for girls with long hair – I was certain to be chosen. My hair was the longest in the class. She started picking girls and didn't seem to notice me. She had already picked eight girls and was struggling to find girls with long hair, even shoulder-length hair seemed to be long to her. No matter how straight I sat, no matter how high I put my hand up, no matter how hard I folded my arms, she just didn't see me.

When she had finished choosing, I remember wishing I could disappear. My friend whispered in my ear, 'Don't worry, perhaps she didn't want people with black hair.' But I knew I was different and that my teacher did not appreciate that difference. I would not volunteer for anything with her again.

Tony

These incidents remind me of the time when I learnt that on occasions it is best to learn without involving the teacher at all if possible. I also learnt that systems in place in school can sometimes be turned to your own benefit. I was seven and I had a teacher called Miss Moss. Every afternoon we spent 15 minutes reading quietly. I enjoyed this time as even at that age reading was what I liked to do best. But there was a problem – we were reading through a scheme. We had to read all of the books in this scheme – all stories about different pirates – before we were allowed free choice from the library. One afternoon I thought I would check the reason with Miss Moss.

Young Tony: 'Miss Moss, please can I go to the library to get a reading book?'
Miss M: 'Have you finished all the Pirate books?'
Young Tony: 'No, I still have to read the Red Pirate, the Blue Pirate and the Green Pirate.'
Miss M: 'Well, once you have read those you can be on free choice.'
Young Tony: 'But Miss, I *can* read.'
Miss M: 'That's not the point. You need to finish the scheme – sit down and read the Red Pirate, then come back and show me.'
Young Tony: 'But Miss, there aren't any Red Pirate books left. Could I read the Green Pirate and then come back to the Red Pirate.'
Miss M: 'SIT DOWN and wait quietly for someone to finish.'

So I sat down, waited quietly until . . . someone finished.

Next afternoon when calling the register, we got to my name.

'Anthony Cotton.'

'Yes, Miss Moose'. Laugher from the whole class – a giggle from me.

'Pardon'.

'Yes, Miss Moose.' More laughter, a little muted this time. Had I pushed it too far?

'Get out until you can be more sensible.'

I left the room with my best 'I don't care' look on my face, and went into the library which is where we got sent out to. I had found a way to get 'free choice' without having to read all the Pirate books. I had also found a way to get a bit of peace and quiet, and time to read a book, whenever I needed it.

I probably retell this story partly through bravado. Of course, not all students win through. I recently had a conversation with a pupil who was in a bottom set for mathematics and was therefore entered for an exam at which the best he could achieve was a 'D' grade. I was amazed that he was in this group as he was clearly capable of much more. He explained how when he was in Year 9 he had messed about during a test and been sent out of the room. He was told afterwards that this was the test which would be used to decide which set the pupils went into for their examination years. He admitted to messing about but said it wasn't fair because the punishment, which clearly seriously affected his whole future, was far too harsh. This petty act of retribution from the teacher means he will have to spend an extra year in college working for a GCSE he could have completed in school.

Another incident which has stayed with me is the day I collected my son at the end of his first day in primary school. I ran to meet him in the playground and didn't understand why he looked so worried. I asked him if he was OK. He nodded. 'But how did you get over the line?' he asked. I didn't understand at first and then realised that there was a white line painted across the playground, and a sign asking all parents to wait behind the line. I had broken the rules and he was frightened that we would both get into trouble. I tried to make a joke of it by jumping from one side of the line to the other with him, but he simply wanted to get away as quickly as possible. He did not want us to challenge this rule. How different from my step-daughter's school, in which many parents make their way to the classroom to collect their children and, if needed, can have a brief conversation with the teacher. I wonder which system makes for a better education?

Marc

I was in a Latin lesson, as I remember I was 13 at the time. (Yes, there are still people alive who had Latin lessons.) The teacher, a sarcastic bully, having established very publicly that a certain individual did not know what a noun phrase was, asked the class for an answer. It was an open question aimed at no one in particular, and with a very particular purpose in mind. About 15 hands went up. I was chosen and began to explain in some detail, naively thinking that the intention was to enlighten my pupil colleague so that he would be able to use noun phrases in future.

'A sentence is divided into . . .,' I started.

'Oh, do shut up,' Sir said dismissively, and waved his hand at someone else who trotted out the tick box answer.

'Stands for a noun, Sir,' he said, looking a little smugly in my direction.

Mission accomplished for the teacher – the stake of failure driven even further into a pupil who already felt stupid. He was now humiliated in front of the rest of the class as well as shown up as ignorant. I too had been put in my place – the classroom was not the place for detailed explanation, at least not by the pupils. This was the teacher's job – the pupils' role to bark quick answers in response.

How much better if the teacher had used this episode as a chance to review noun phrases, to find out how many of the pupils with their hands still had not fully grasped 'noun phrases', or even to use the pupils' knowledge to help out our colleague and support his learning. But no, this teacher took up the time with unskilled questioning in order to ritually humiliate a 13-year-old. Not something which a teacher should aspire to.

Vicky

Although many of the group seemed to have clear memories of teachers they had disliked with a passion during their own time at school, I was reminded of an incident much more recent, an incident which shows that even if teachers and schools are supportive and caring children may still be experiencing fear and humiliation.

My own daughter started to be afraid of school. The school she was attending is open, friendly and receptive but I felt I did not know who to turn to for help. I still felt new to the school and unfamiliar with the way that the school system works. My initial reaction was to feel extremely 'anti' everything to do with the school and give my daughter a break. However, even after a few days off school her fears continued and began to manifest themselves outwardly as nervous obsessions which completely affected her character. At this point I realised that we both needed support.

I bumped into a teacher who remarked on her behaviour. 'What has happened? It's like she's a different person.' I took this to heart and began talking to certain teachers in the school I felt comfortable with. They took notice of what I was saying and gave me time. Until then I had thought that no one considered it important enough to deal with; it seemed to be sort of shrugged off. After all, there is always someone with worse problems than you.

Four years later it emerged that the problem was due to bullying. A child in my daughter's class threatened not to 'be her friend' if she did not do certain things with her, such as stealing from other people's lunch boxes, putting a jumper down the toilet and sitting with her at lunch time. My daughter knew this was wrong and tried every way she could to avoid this loyalty test. The best way she thought she could get out of the situation was to avoid lunch times altogether. She begged to be home dinners – this was impossible, however, the teacher let my daughter eat her lunch in the classroom on her own, which at first seemed to help. However, for the next three years her fear of lunch times remained. At its worst she would worry every morning that strange objects were about to leap out of her lunch box – like guns or monsters. As a parent I could not help but be annoyed – why hadn't anyone noticed the intimidation from the girl in the class and how it was affecting her?

We still talk about this situation and my daughter reminds us how helpful it is to talk about our worries. So, as a parent, I want to ask all teachers to make time for the fearful children they will inevitably come across. Talk to the parents and talk to the child: you may well be the first person to come across the problem. I asked my daughter if she would mind if I wrote about this episode. She thought it would be good to tell people who want to be teachers about it. As a teacher you try to understand individuals' needs however odd they may seem. Just being told to stop being silly did not help my daughter, neither did simply giving her a hug. Only by attempting to see through the situation were we able to sort it out.

Reflection

Your first reaction on reading this chapter may be to think things like this don't happen any more. However, we all shared very recent memories which made us ashamed to be involved in education. Tony and Vicky both tell of very recent incidents with their own children which made them question the wisdom of teachers. If two people who obviously are close to education and schools can feel threatened by schools, what feelings must many other parents have about teaching and teachers?

One purpose of writing this chapter is to help you think through what your reaction would be to teachers who behave in a way you may feel is inappropriate. What would you do if you were placed in a position on teaching practice in which your mentor regularly tore up pupils' work which they did not deem satisfactory. This happened recently to one of Tony's student teachers.

Both James and Helen have clear memories of times when they were humiliated in class; a public humiliation, which led to them feeling inadequate, angry and confused. The incidents they relate have not helped them become better people by being exposed to the harsh realities of life. These events deeply affected the way they viewed schools, teaching, and themselves for many years. The incident with Miss Moss is an example of a teacher sticking to a routine even when it does not make educational sense; sticking to the rule simply because it is a rule, rather than thinking will it help children to learn. Marc's Latin teacher was more interested in maintaining his control than effective teaching and Jasbir's teacher ensure that she lost a willing and able learner through her own prejudices.

The role of teacher is obviously a very important one. What may seem like a minor incident to us as a teacher may remain with our pupils for the rest of their lives. As teachers we have a choice of the kinds of memories of school we would like pupils to take away with them, and of the images of themselves that we help to create. Teachers do make a difference, they are important people to their learners.

A good teacher offers a child faith in themselves, faith in education, security and trust. Being a good teacher means you can enable pupils in your care to cope with any unfairness which they may come across in the rest of their time in schools and even later in life.

Questions for your journal

As you begin to work in classrooms you may become frustrated by some pupils you work with. They may seem to moan about anything you do. You may feel as though nothing you do can satisfy them. If this happens then revisit this part of your journal. It may help you see things from their point of view. It may help you find ways of sorting the situation out so that both you and the child come to value each others' time and company.

- Write about a time you remember when a teacher was unfair either to you or to a friend. Add as much detail as you can.
- What does this incident tell you about school?
- How did it make you feel?
- What would you have liked the teacher to have done?
- What would you do now in the same situation?
- What do you wish you had done at the time?
- Was there a time at school when you felt afraid?
- What could a teacher have done to support you at this time?
- Think about a teacher who was particularly ineffective in your time at school. What steps could they have taken to improve your learning?

Chapter 4

Careers Advice

Introduction

This chapter may seem slightly unusual at first glance. We did not set out with the intention of writing a chapter on careers advice but Dorothy's story struck a chord with the group. Dorothy described a career adviser who she only saw once but who, with a few casually uttered words, significantly altered her thinking and her life plan. We suddenly realised how important all our actions as teachers are, even those actions we may not notice at the time.

The most striking element of the following stories is how very casually most of the advice was given. The storytellers recount advice given in passing as a teacher walked by; spur of the moment decisions made on their behalf by a teacher who felt that they knew best, and didactic sessions in which the careers adviser completely took over and chose their path for them.

The stories also show that careers advice can come from many angles and in many unexpected ways. Very few of the advice sessions recounted were actually conducted by proper careers advisers in a formal setting. Instead, advice came from parents, teachers, community workers and friends, sometimes when least expected. However, all of the stories have a common theme in that the advice given was in time to have a significant bearing on the career path of the authors.

Dorothy

The story around my one and only careers advice session at school is one which I have often retold and used as an illustration on training courses. However, this does not detract from the pain and bitterness that this episode caused me then. These feelings are still evoked now, more than 20 years later, no matter how laughingly I tell the story. This moment was to be seminal in developing my attitude to education and my personal definition of racism.

As Year 10 pupils we had been told that we were to have a 15-minute careers advice sessions which would help us decide what path we might follow on leaving school. The point of the session was to discuss the finer details of possible career choices with an objective adult and I was looking forward to doing so and receiving some guidance. Another attraction was that the interview meant 15 minutes away from the classroom!

I was scheduled to follow my best friend, Jane, and so waited excitedly for her to return from her session so I could find out what she had been told. We were following exactly the same O levels so I knew that whatever advice had been offered to her should apply to me also. I fiddled with the hem of my stiff and unbecoming grey school skirt and looked critically at the awful sludge green 'Peter Pan' collar blouse and thick grey blazer that comprised the rest of the uniform along with the regulation footwear. I thought with glee about starting work and being able to consign those awful clothes to the bin. Perhaps, I thought, I would substitute one uniform for another. I had always wanted to be a nurse and imagined myself in a crisp, rustling white uniform. What exactly would I be wearing as I went out into the big wide working world?

My reverie was interrupted by Jane emerging from the classroom which had been temporarily converted into the 'careers office'. I pounced on her, eager to hear her report. 'What did he say, what did he say?' Her reply was nonchalant; he had been pleased to hear that she was doing eight O levels and had suggested that she stay on to do A levels and then go to university, perhaps even on to postgraduate study. Jane had told him she didn't want to do this as she was going to join the WRENS and she didn't need A levels for this. My eyes were as big as saucers. A levels! A degree! Even postgraduate studies – whatever they were. Despite being in the top stream at school it had never been suggested that I should stay on into the sixth form. This rare honour was reserved for a few and we thought they had already been singled out – was I about to join this elite group? Here was someone from outside school who as about to give me hope. I was practically hugging myself with glee as I awaited his call.

Finally, my moment came. I entered the makeshift careers office and found myself face to face with a middle aged, white man. He asked me how many O levels I was doing and in what subjects. I told him. He looked at me for what seemed like an age. 'Eight O levels is quite impressive.' A pause. 'Have you ever thought about taking a job in Woolworths. You may have to start at the checkout tills but if you work hard you could rise to the rank of supervisor.' I cannot remember how I answered him. Perhaps I didn't say anything. All I know is that I was deeply shocked and numbed by his words. He must have said other things but I heard nothing else from that moment. I became aware of the hard, uncomfortable school chair I was sitting on and felt a part of me shrivel up and die inside. My friend had been told to aspire to a Masters' degree. I had been told to aspire to a supervisor's position in Woolworths.

I left the room after what seemed an age. Jane was outside waiting for me as eagerly as I had waited for her. She fluttered about me asking as I had done, 'What did he say, what did he say?' I told her. She looked shocked and then laughed nervously. I wanted to cry but I didn't, either then or later. The pain I felt was too great for crying. Jane was deeply embarrassed by the advice I had been offered and by my subsequent emotions. We never discussed it again.

So, why was Jane pushed towards a life of academia and its subsequent rewards whilst I was guided towards the sweet counter in Woolworths? Perhaps the answer is not so simple as the one I am about to give, but in 20 years of reflection I have not been able to come up with a better one. Jane is white, I am Black.

I remember how much faith we had in this 'careers adviser'. We had looked forward to the session as if he had a crystal ball in which the mists would clear to reveal to him our futures. So this session had a profound impact on me. It caused me to doubt myself and lose confidence. It shook my belief in my mother's words. 'You can be whatever you want to be.' The incident also made me acutely aware of institutional racism. Here was a member of the establishment slapping me down for daring to believe that the only Black girl in the O level group could have the same aspirations as her peers. Of course I was already aware of racism – name calling, insults and even physical attacks were commonplace – but this was the first time I became aware of the self-fulfilling prophecy which conspires in the failure of Black and other children. It felt like an unequal battle between my mother saying, 'You can succeed' and the forces of authority saying, 'Know your place and don't step out of it.'

I became demotivated. If I was destined for Woolworths there was no need to work hard. My grades suffered, I hung out with other equally disillusioned kids, cheeked teachers, played truant. I dropped from the O level group into the CSE set in two subjects, this serving to increase my alienation from school. This went on for some time until I realised that I was simply conforming to stereotype. The turning point came with the end of year report. My mother wanted to know why my grades had fallen so far. I broke down and told her of the hopelessness and helplessness I felt. How I felt consigned to someone else's scrapheap. She explained that the point of trying was not for anyone else, not even her. I had to try for myself. If I really cared about myself I would ignore the low expectations of others and work towards my own goals. I picked up my studies, worked hard, and gained six O levels and a clutch of CSEs. Perhaps I ought to thank the careers adviser; he taught me to set my own goals and not to be content with those set for me by others.

Helen

"I remember a different form of careers advice, but it was an experience which transformed my life in a similar way. I had an interview with one of the deputy heads after my success at A levels. It was a deputy head I did not know and about whom I can remember nothing. All I remember is the following exchange:

Deputy head: 'So, why don't you want to go to university?'
Helen: 'I've got into Teacher Training College.'
Deputy head: 'And are you happy with that.'
Helen: 'Well, yes,' (Unconvinced)
Deputy head: 'You see, your results are much better than we expected, which means you could get a place at university.'
Helen: 'But I've got a place at Teacher Training College. I couldn't go somewhere else now.'
Deputy head: 'Why not? It happens all the time.'
Helen: 'But how could I get in now – it's too late.'
Deputy head: 'Look, where do you want to go.'
Helen: 'Well, somewhere near York, I suppose. That's where my boyfriend's going.'
Deputy head: 'Let's try York them.'
Helen: 'No, I've heard you need straight As to get there.'
Deputy head: 'OK, let's try somewhere near York then.'

At this point he picked up the phone, glanced through a book in front of him and dialled. 'Hello, Sheffield University English Department? I've got a girl here ...' A little later, he put the phone down and turned to me.

'Well, that's sorted then. all you have to do is wait for the form they are sending and send it straight back.'

'But, my mum doesn't know ... What shall I say in the letter to the Teacher Training College? Where will I stay? When will I start ... ?'

'Well done, Helen. You would have been so bored at that college. Good luck for the future. Next!'

Tony

"I have a kind of half memory of an interview to decide A level choices. I do not know who it was with, where it was or at what stage of the school year it took place. I do remember entering the room convinced that I wanted to study history, English and maths at A level, and in that order. I loved history and English. My friends had all chosen these two subjects with another arts subject. I had chosen maths because that is the subject I was best at. I left the room having been told that I would take maths, further maths and physics. After all, I was a boy and so I would be better at the sciences, especially with my talent in maths. I would also find, I was told, a wider range of career choices by opting for the sciences. (It was also impossible for me to mix arts subjects and science subjects because of the timetable.)

Vicky

I really do not remember any formal careers advice. I do remember a big green book at home, a bit like a bible. My mother showed it to me one evening. I took it to bed and looked up all the subjects I was thinking of opting for at school and concluded that my ideal career was as a window dresser. As always I seemed to talk myself out of that career fairly quickly, although I recently realised my window dressing vision with a display in a Mencap shop of the work from one of my groups.

I do have a memory of an English teacher coming up to me at break time at the end of my fifth year at secondary school and asking me what I was going to do. I just shrugged my shoulders. She suggested that I might want to 'carry on in education'. She seemed almost disappointed that I had even thought I wouldn't. That very fleeting and informal moment did make me think about it, however. It reminded me of all the things I didn't want to do and offered a possible way forward to find something I did want to do. From that day all I wanted to do was finish my O levels and be out of school for ever. I found the whole process of taking exams so awful that I vowed I would never take any ever again. I have managed to stick to this vow – so far!

Marc

Although I do not remember much about being offered careers advice myself, I do remember an incident which reminded me of the role we play as teachers in influencing our students after they leave use. At the end of a particularly difficult day at school I was walking home, slowly, so that I could avoid entering the house with a visible black cloud over my head. On the way I met an ex-student who I had not seen since she left school 12 months previously. She was a student I had resigned myself to being disliked by. We had several run-ins – she was very clever but had been in great danger of doing very badly in her exams. I had felt she was getting away with too much in many of her classes, and had not been prepared to put up with it in mine. I though all I might get was a brief, ' 'lo, Sir', but she was pleased to see me, and wanted to tell me what she was up to. She made it clear during our conversation that she was grateful for the work I had done as her teacher, talked a little about the difficulties of Asian girls leaving home to go to university and made a big show of telling her boyfriend I was a really good teacher. I laughed, and she, very seriously, told me I *was* a good teacher. I walked the rest of the way home transformed.

Reflection

In some of these stories we see 'men in suits' wielding the big stick of stereotypical expectations and forcing young people to drink from the prescribed water. The young people here seem helpless in the face of someone who has 'The Knowledge'. Dorothy's bitter but bold fight for what *she* wanted is a sign that many young people in the writers' generation had to fight to have any control over their career paths.

Of course, things today will be very different, but there are some fundamental points we need to consider as teachers with a direct influence over our students' futures. Becoming sensitive to the way young people display their anticipation, nerves and excitement about learning, and the possibilities attached to that learning, must be a key part of any teacher's job. We need to know and understand the people we are influencing if we are to take this responsibility seriously.

Marc's story illustrates several dilemmas for teachers. Firstly, everyone likes to be liked, and sometimes the responsibilities of the job require actions which result in you *not* being liked. Secondly the 'good' and the 'liked' issues are often confused. You may be told what a great teacher you are by students whose judgements on such matters you cannot give any weight to; they may be to divert your focus from something they have done (or are thinking of doing). Equally, you will go through hell with some students who, on leaving school, will thank you genuinely and warmly for your support.

We model our attitude towards learning in our every response and action around school and we must make certain these positive messages are available for all. Even a casual comment can become an important influence on a confused young person, who doesn't feel they know enough about themselves to make the best life-changing choices. Any strength of personality can be made into a positive opportunity for comment, reasoning the student about their capabilities and reinforcing their sense of self.

Our students face many and varied pressures in our education system, and a few will resist all our best efforts to make a difference in their life choices. It is much more likely that we, as teachers and as human beings, will exert a great deal of influence on our students' futures. Our main responsibility must be to ensure this influence is relevant and positive. It is a responsibility too. We must strike a balance between abdicating this responsibility as Vicky's teachers chose to do, or completely dominating the future lives of our pupils as Helen's deputy head did. We must also try to be flexible in the choices we offer, not allowing school timetables or prejudices to push individuals down paths simply because they are administratively simple or fit institutional or personal views of aptitude to future employment prospects.

Questions for your journal

You probably have an image of yourself as a teacher of a subject which you hold dear and which excites you. But teachers are so much more to so many pupils. This section of your journal offers you a way of starting to think about the other ways in which you will be viewed by pupils. It also asks you to reflect on the huge responsibility which accompanies the job. You are literally in a position which for some pupils can be life changing.

- How have you made decisions about your career in the past?
- Can you remember when you decided you wanted to become a teacher?
- Who influenced you?
- Can you think of other incidents which have affected your life choices?
- What would you do if you didn't become a teacher?
- What advice do you wish you had been given when you were still at school?
- What do you think is the best form of careers advice you will be able to offer?

Chapter 5

Expectations and Motivation

Introduction

We are all motivated to succeed in one way or another, otherwise we would not have written this book and you would not be reading it. However, this motivation can come from many different sources. On some occasions we aim to meet ambitions others have for us, on other occasions we may fight to overcome obstacles others have put in our way. We want to do well to show those who did not have faith in us what we are really capable of, as well as to repay the faith of those who always expected us to do well.

The two great motivators you will read about in this chapter are teachers and families. As a teacher you need to be able to motivate all your learners, even those who seem to care little about learning. It is not enough to blame their lack of motivation for their failure. It is your job to find ways to teach them. It is also a teacher's job to find out about the supports and obstacles which the pupils bring with them to school. Our aim is that the following anecdotes will make these difficult tasks more transparent.

You will also read about expectations. Either expectations which others had of the authors or expectations the authors had of school. The anecdotes show how important expectations are for the self-image of learners in schools.

Jasbir

When I think of my school days, the memory of my family wanting me to do well is very clear. My brother who was 18 years older than me would say, 'Well, I want to have a sister I can be proud of.' My mother would say if I didn't work hard and 'do well' there would be no choice for me but to get married. My dad was the one who didn't put any pressure on me but there was still an expectation that I would succeed.

I had no way of knowing if I was doing well until I started secondary school and we had our first exams. I came second in the class. In the same way, my family were never sure how 'well' I was doing at school. My parents rarely attended parents' evenings as my mum did not speak English very well and my dad and brother worked night shifts. At the time they assumed you only went into your child's school if there was an problem. I was quite happy that they didn't come into school. It was a way I could keep the two parts of my life separate. At that time a lot of Asian families like mine did not really understand the British school system and probably a lot of families still don't.

I continued to do well in my exams and my family were happy with the reports of my success. One evening I realised how my mother did not really understand how well I was doing. She said to me, 'Seva's daughter is really clever, she has got three O levels.' she had no idea what I was doing at school. I remember laughing and explaining that I was about to take eight O levels. From that point onwards my mother put a lot of energy into finding out what I was really doing – 'What next?' 'What if . . .' – and making sure I had the support to continue and to succeed. Having to discuss what I was doing was really useful as it made me think through for myself the reasons I had chosen particular subjects and not others. I guess my best careers adviser was my mum.

I have said my mum didn't quite understand the school system. Well, on occasions I think I didn't understand it either. As a child I remember being told to stand in the corner because I had been talking whilst the teacher had been reading a story. I must have been about five years old and when I was told to go to the corner I didn't realise I had done anything wrong and didn't realise being sent to the corner was a punishment. I remember shaking my head and saying, 'No, thank you' to the teacher, 'I would rather stay where I am.' She seemed to be quite cross so I thought I had better move. She carried on reading the story and as I couldn't really hear very well my attention began to wander; it rested on the books on display and I decided to go and have a look. Suddenly the teacher became even angrier and I began to cry. I don't know what happened after that apart from feelings of confusion and not wanting to be there. This incident remains with me as I am reminded of it daily. On many occasions when children are sent to me as headteacher they appear unclear about why they are being punished and what they have done wrong. Children need to understand the rules we make in school and very young children especially need to talk through what is acceptable behaviour not once but many times.

Dorothy

My motivation to succeed came initially from my mother and then much later from my own overriding desire to do well. My mother left school early without any qualifications as her family could not afford to keep her in school. She felt this bitterly and resolved that her five children would finish school and go on to further vocational education. She was very ambitious for us and did not want us to end up in low-paid jobs without prospects of promotion of advancement and felt that education was the only way to prevent this.

However, my mother did not understand the British school system as she had moved to England only three years before I started school. She had a deep and abiding faith in the teachers and found it difficult to accept my assertions that some teachers were racist in their dealings with me and that this sometimes made learning difficult. She was also unfamiliar with the UK standards of education, especially when I began O levels, therefore she had no yardstick against which to measure my progress. So, she left choices such as which O levels to take entirely up to me. I ended up choosing O levels in subjects I liked rather than those which would help future career choices. However, this gave me the motivation to succeed and to this day much of my academic success stems from the fact that I have always studied areas which I enjoy.

Succeeding now seems like a way of repaying the faith my mother had in us. A way of showing that the struggle, including a 5,000 mile relocation, was worth it. Succeeding is also a way of ensuring that my children will not have to fight the same battles, as much of the ground will have already been prepared for them.

James

I had passed the 11+ and had to travel to grammar school from the London borough in which I lived. On my first day at school I realised that everyone else seemed to know a whole group of friends. I seemed to be the only one who didn't have a group of friends. However, I slowly began to become a part of a group of 'outcasts'. This grouping took place through bus routes. In fact, some of the group radically altered their travel routes so that after a while we were all travelling into school together. The group grew closer and closer, doing everything together and gaining a reputation for being troublemakers. I remember the head of the first year calling us all into his office to tell us that this was the first time he had ever had such problems with a group of pupils. We took a kind of pride in this label and often tried to live up to it. We even christened ourselves 'The Magnificent Thirteen'. There was never any space for new members. We were a closed group with a strict code of indiscipline.

The group gave me the security I needed for a while but eventually I wanted more. I remember that for once I found myself actually concentrating in class. As I listened to the teacher questioning the group I realised that I knew an answer. I was suddenly forced to make a decision. As a member of 'The Magnificent Thirteen' I had taken our set of vows. One of these pledges was that we would never answer a question in class. But for some reason, on this occasion, I wanted to answer. I took the plunge and answered, correctly. It was almost as if the teacher sensed change, it was if they visibly relaxed. However, as soon as I answered I looked back down at my desk – I did not dare meet the gaze of any other member of 'The Magnificent Thirteen'. When we left the class all hell broke loose. I was teased and ridiculed: it was as if I had betrayed a trust, as if I had changed sides.

We eventually patched up our differences as a group. It was our turn to lighten up. It was this, perhaps, that led us all to places in the 'A' stream and eventually the sixth form. In fact, later on during football trials some of the group were selected and some were not. There was no antagonism within the group. We still needed security from those we felt comfortable with, but also valued our differences.

Helen

I was at work in a factory making roller towel machines on the day the A level results came through, not daring to take a day off work to collect my results in case I had failed them all. Just before the morning break my name and my results were broadcast over the tannoy by the shopfloor manager and my stomach churned. My mum had done what she said she wouldn't – she had opened the results and rung in to tell me.

My excitement at my unexpected success lasted minutes as the eldest of the women workers turned to me and said. 'A for English, B for History and C for some 'ology. She'll think she is above us now.' How ironic that I was blamed here for success, when all the pressure I had felt at school was about failing.

Until that moment I'd been tolerated as a necessary part of the seasonally expanded workforce. After my success in a system which had denied success to most of my work colleagues, I was outcast and spent a few miserable weeks in isolation. I was, after all, a council house girl whose mum was a barmaid What did I think I was doing over-reaching myself like that? Despite the pride in my mum which led to her making the phone call, part of her didn't want me to be the first member of the family to go to university. To her, this meant I would grow away from her and lose contact with my roots.

Tony

As a child of 11 I was taught in the 'top' group in my primary school. On Fridays we had a mental arithmetic test. The child who scored highest in the test sat in desk 1 (next to the teacher) for the following week, the child 'coming second' sat in the next desk, and so on. After a week or two I realised that by getting two or three questions wrong I would be about fifth in the test and get to sit by the door. This had at least two advantages. I wasn't always under the nose of the teacher, and I was first out of the door to get in the queue for the sticky buns we were able to buy every morning play time. I could engineer this result as I was confident that I knew all the correct answers and so could deliberately make my two or three errors. When I look back I can see that my confidence and skill in mathematics carried with it a particular power. I knew I could do well at maths if I wanted to, so when it really mattered, when my parents would find out or in end of year exams, I could perform to the best of my ability. On other occasions I would do as well as I *needed* to. I also think that part of the reason I behaved in this way was to frustrate the teachers. It almost felt like I was getting one over on them by not doing as well as they expected. A teacher on a course brought this memory to the front of my mind when she told of a similar experience, although her experience had left her feeling powerless and out of control. She felt she could not 'do' mathematics. Fridays brought with them anxiety and panic. She knew she would do badly in the test, would be made to sit in a 'lower' desk and worst of all, that her mother would see she had failed when she collected her after school.

I was, however, brought down to earth with a bump on one occasion. I had been asked to read a story out loud which I had been working on. This story was about an escaped convict. I had named the convict James Hesketh in my story. I felt mischievous as I approached the section of the story in which the convict was discovered. Not only was Mr Hesketh our teacher, but his first name was James, and we were never supposed to know our teachers' first names, let alone speak them out loud. As I read out the name, the whole class seemed to recognise I had overstepped the mark. I was called out to the front desk and we went through the motions which preceded getting the cane, which occasionally still happened in this class. I remember the cane swishing through the air, I remember the desk being caned, but I can't remember whether I was actually caned or not. Much worse than this, I was told that from that moment I would have to go and work in the next group down; I was no longer a member of 4A1, I was banished to 4A2. I realised the seriousness of this: the kids in 4A1 would almost all pass the 11+ and go on to grammar school, while none of the kids in 4A2 would pass the 11+. In 4A1 we were groomed for the test and we often sat mock papers. None of this happened in 4A2. I went home that night, not daring to tell my parents what had happened, even though I sensed they would see the trivial nature of my offence. It would be too difficult to cope with the fuss. I had learnt where the real power lay in that classroom, so I worked hard in 4A2 and fairly quickly was moved back into 4A1.

Reflection

How do we learn the rules of the game for success at school? Native cunning? Social pressures? Trial and error? As we know, not all students do learn how to succeed at school. In England today there are approximately 11,000 permanently excluded students, mostly boys, currently at large and mostly unsupported. For this reason alone it is worth examining how we can motivate students to want to do well at school, to convince those who are not initially interested that this learning business is actually worthwhile.

However, the stories here show that success brings its own problems for many children. We see James riding a tightrope between success in the classroom and alienation from his peers, and Tony more concerned about sticky buns than the possibility of being seen to be successful in mental arithmetic. Again, peer acceptance is more important than academic achievement. We also read about the positive nature of peer groups, the support and gentle competition they can offer; perhaps as teachers we need to find ways of working with the groups which pupils choose to operate in rather than imposing our own groupings. These groups can counteract the alienation which some pupils feel within schools. Indeed, schools which do not consciously work to avoid discrimination can perpetuate the racism and prejudice against working-class pupils described by Jasbir, Dorothy and James.

Throughout the chapter success has been interpreted as doing well in exams; interesting in itself, even if the individual measures of this success are varied. Academic achievement is even more important now than it was for the authors. The number of jobs for unskilled workers is reducing, as is the comparative pay for such jobs. The consequences of failing to learn how to succeed in school are potentially far more serious and one-way. For educators the difficulty is how to describe the mountain some students have to climb without putting them off before they make the first step?

One answer is to provide students with success. They need to know clearly what they have to do to achieve success, and teachers must be ready to reward success flexibly and fairly. All of the contributors had occasions when they saw what personal actions they had to take if they were to achieve their goals. These actions were supported either by parents or by teachers, whose encouragement made success possible, but in the end it was down to us as individuals to take a decision which occasionally isolated us from people we had regarded as friends or colleagues.

(Support was necessary here, too!) We had been introduced to the idea of success at an early stage and had begun to establish our own questions and doubts from an early age. There are clear implications for primary teachers. How can they be more explicit about 'the rules of the game'? How can they encourage children to begin to question, as well as equip them with the basic skills necessary for success? In a similar way all teachers need to find ways of ensuring that parents, carers and learners are clear how success is measured. We all need to know if and when we are doing well.

Parents figure large in most of our stories: Jasbir's parents wanting her to do well but being unsure how to operate within a system they felt excluded from; Dorothy's mother having an ambition for her which she saw then, as she does now, as supportive and enabling. Unfortunately parental ambitions here were squashed by an unresponsive school. In contrast Tony tells the story of a child frightened of failure because of the repercussions this may have at home. On occasions education is an area where even the most well-meaning parent and teacher may have a blind spot. We may overemphasise what was important in our own education; take for granted what we saw as good without questioning its relevance to our children. Perhaps teachers in their role as *in loco parentis* need to avoid these traps too.

It appears that success in school, for the authors, came through learning the rules of the game in order to do what we wanted, although when teachers are not clear about what these rules are, as in Tony's case, this can lead to pupils challenging a system in negative ways rather than focusing their energy on positive behaviour. Within a particular teacher's lesson the authors developed an understanding of that teacher's behaviour, and responded to it in the way that served them best. As teachers we can build on this through well-planned, relevant, skilfully taught lessons. Much harder to teach are the students who do not want to learn the rules of the game, and who have no particular end in mind for themselves. If they are not part of the game, it is very difficult to play it with them. Perhaps as teachers the best we can do is be honest with our pupils. Be clear with them when they are succeeding and equally clear when things aren't going so well, offering advice and support in order to move beyond the immediate difficulty. It is not enough to leave pupils to get on, blissfully unaware that they are engaged in mundane activity which will not lead to future success. We must work hard with our pupils so that they come to know what success means for themselves.

New teachers have to make a decision about how formal their relationship with their students will be. Some teachers would have shrugged off Tony's use of their first name; indeed in some schools today the use of teachers' first names by pupils is the norm. Some years ago a student teacher did two teaching practices, one in a school in which students *had* to use first names when talking to staff, whereas the mere mention of this possibility in the second brought the entire staff room to a halt and resulted in a 'quiet word' to the student. Tony may have been simply testing the system, but in all classrooms this is something we need to have thought through for ourselves. If we call a student 'Mita', why do we expect her to call us 'Sir' or 'Miss'? As our relationships with students are at the core of our effectiveness as teachers, we do well to have clear answers ready when the students ask, as they always will, 'What's your first name Sir?' or 'Why do we have to call you Sir, Sir?'

Questions for your journal

On the day you come home from school scratching your head and asking that question, 'How do you motivate those pupils who just don't want to learn?' you can read this section of your journal. You were not always the model pupil. There will have been times when a teacher will have gone home wondering how on earth they could interest you in their subject. What could they have done to gain your interest? What was it that switched you off and what could have switched you on? Maybe working on these questions will offer you some way forward.

- What gave you the will to succeed?
- What affected this will to succeed, both positively and negatively?
- List all the different reasons you can think of for doing well at school.
- Which of these reasons can teachers make most impact on?
- How can teachers motivate children who have such different reasons to want to do well?

Part 3

Experiences in Education as Teachers

Overview

So far the book has predominantly focused on our experiences as children in education. This experience is not insignificant. After all most of us have spent more time in education as pupils or students than in any other role. So clearly this time of our lives will have had a great effect on what we become when we switch roles and are suddenly the ones called 'teacher'. It is no surprise that beginning teachers often feel closer to the pupils they are teaching than the colleagues they are supposed to be working with. You will all feel slightly odd the first time you enter the staff room without knocking. You may even have a feeling of changing sides. But it is important to look at things from teachers' points of view as well as from pupils' perspectives. After all you are going to be a teacher.

There is a difference between reflecting on ourselves as learners and becoming a teacher who acts on these memories. In some ways it is more difficult to learn from other people than it is to learn from ourselves. We know why we behaved in particular ways, we can even sometimes understand what we wish we had done differently. We often have a hunch about what might happen if we change our behaviour. But all of this becomes much more difficult when trying to learn from others' practice. It is not simply a matter of seeing what works for somebody else, or of endlessly repeating sessions that worked as one-offs for us. Unfortunately, it is much more difficult than that. What we must try to do is understand the trick of turning other peoples' good practice into our own practice. Genuinely our own practice, too, not simply copying moves that others make. We need to get to the stage when others who watch us don't realise we have learnt this from someone else, but think it is the way we always work: the stage when we have forgotten that we have learnt it from observing others, we just do it, for example when we don't have to think about changing gear in a car, or what to do first when we tie our shoelaces. On the way to this fluency we will have adapted what we observed as good practice so that it becomes our own practice.

But before we can learn from other teachers, and before we can notice what is successful in our own practice we need to learn how to observe classrooms. This is incredibly difficult at first. It is difficult to know what to look for and difficult to know what to pick out but gradually things will become clear. A student teacher once said at the end of their one-year Post Graduate Teaching course, 'I've only just learnt how to observe classrooms. If only I'd been able to do this at the beginning of the course I would have done so much better.' Unfortunately there are not really any tricks. It has been said that what we try to do when we observe others is to 'make the familiar strange'. Indeed it is sometimes easier to observe classrooms outside our own *experience or our own subject area as only then do we really begin to notice things. This helps us begin to notice things in classrooms we are more familiar with, which at first appear hidden in the fog of assumed common sense. Observing classrooms outside our own subject area can help us come to question our own common sense.*

So the stories in this section offer you views from many different classrooms, in many different contexts. Some will feel comfortable, normal for you. Other will feel 'strange'. We hope all will make you wonder what you can take out of that episode and how you might use it in your own context. Within this section you will find a whole range of teaching approaches and styles. Perhaps simply being aware of this range of possibilities will help you in observing classrooms. You will recognise some situations as they appear. By reading and reflecting on the situations here, perhaps before you observe a classroom, you may learn the questions to ask both yourself and those you are observing in order to begin to make sense of the classrooms you are observing and working in.

Chapter 6

Watching Others Teach

Introduction

Teachers do not have enough time to watch other teachers teach, but the best way to spread good practice is to watch it in action. For this reason memories of good teachers are precious, memories which can be drawn on for ideas or for a secure point of reference in a busy day.

Watching others teach is also useful because it implicitly invites several questions. Could I have done that better? What specific advice can I give a colleague who wants help? How on earth did they get the pupils to do that? It is often best to watch your colleagues, whether you are just about to start your training or have been teaching for years with a specific focus in mind. This could be the activities of a particular child or group of children, the way the teacher questions the class, the practical organisation in the room, the clarity of the instructions. The questions are endless and each imposes a different role on the observer. You will find such questions coming to mind as you read the descriptions of teachers in this chapter.

The following stories describe good teachers and focus on what the teachers are doing. Do not forget though that good teaching is also obvious from watching what the pupils are doing. If they are confident in the activities they have been set, if they seem to understand what they are supposed to be doing, and most of all if they are excited about doing it, then there is some good teaching going on.

Tony

> It is very easy to think of colleagues who have greatly influenced the way I work, or who have impressed me with their obvious teaching skills but much more difficult to pin down precise moments when these observations have immediately challenged my thinking. However, I can think of two such occasions at the second school I taught in.
>
> On the first occasion I was at the school for interview. I had only been teaching for two years and was nervously sitting in the staff room, feeling

very uncomfortable in my interview suit. You can pick up lots of things from simply observing and listening to teachers in their staff room – their private space. Two young women teachers came into the room. They were obviously teachers of English, and equally obviously one of them had just had a very difficult lesson with some challenging pupils. (I was later to discover that there were a lot of challenging pupils in the school.) However, rather than complaining about the pupils, and blaming the failure of the lesson on the pupils, the two women were having an intense discussion about why the planning of the lesson may have created bad behaviour. What should she do next time to involve this particular pupil? What might have caused this behaviour in him today when he had been fine yesterday?

I remember this as the first time I realised that many teachers genuinely liked their pupils and enjoyed teaching. At my previous school the talk in the staff room had all been of how dreadful the pupils were, how they made it impossible to teach properly and should be punished more. Here, however, were teachers who respected kids, who enjoyed the challenge of helping them learn, and saw it as their job to work with pupils to help them succeed. They saw their pupils as fellow human beings, and saw teaching as a challenging, yet immensely rewarding job. I decided immediately that I wanted to work in that school, and with teachers like these two.

I was successful in the interview and taught at the school for five years. Many of the teachers have become role models for me. Another lesson, or fragment of a lesson, I remember clearly as having a huge impact was when I accidentally stumbled into the beginning of an art lesson. The teacher was a friend, and I had often wondered how he might work with kids, but with him being down in the art room I didn't often pass his way. (Looking back I realise how narrow-minded it was of me not to make the effort – I have often learnt most from watching teachers at work in different subject areas to my own.) Ted was working with a group of pupils, many of whom I recognised from one of my more difficult maths groups. He had them all gathered around the front bench and was explaining a particular art technique to them using a large print of a well-known painting. This may not sound at all unusual. What was unusual was the way he was using language, using all the technical vocabulary without checking that they understood what the words meant; he assumed they would follow, and they did. I learnt a very quick lesson about expectations. It seemed to me that often in my mathematics lessons I must come over as extremely patronising, always checking that everybody knew the meaning of technical vocabulary and thinking of ways of simplifying my explanations. Ted did the opposite. He used the technical vocabulary, but in a context where it made sense, and through using such vocabulary in an everyday way the kids understood the language in the context in which it was normally used. They also were being talked to as artists, rather than as children learning to be artists, which gave them an image of themselves as doers of art not learners of art. I have tried since then to offer a view of myself and my pupils as mathematicians rather than learners of mathematics and, rather than simplifying vocabulary, I find situations to introduce the vocabulary in which the meaning can be seen.

I was reminded of the importance of expectation, and the skill of maintaining high expectations in a lesson I observed recently. These are my lesson observation notes,

All change this morning. The new(ish) head of maths is teaching two groups together with the other class teacher as support. A long thin classroom has been created by removing a partition and the classroom contains 53 pupils and two teachers. The lesson begins by exploring negative numbers. Several pupils give a summary of 'what we looked at last time'. These pupils are selected by name – not by hands up. Each pupil offers a suggestion, which is developed by the teacher and the next pupil he engages in the exchange. After this discussion the class is reminded of all the real contexts in which we see negative numbers: thermometers, temperature, golf, and so on. I can't help noticing that the teacher speaks in a fairly broad accent, which matches that of most of the pupils – I wonder if this helps give the pupils confidence and trust in him? He often uses the phase, 'Yes, we are all happy with this' to signal that he knows implicitly that everyone is capable of following what is being discussed.

He then asks pupils to come up to the board on which he has drawn a pair of axes; again he asks by name, there is no putting up of hands. Also noticeable is that no child fails to carry out the task, and no child complains about coming out to the board. When the diagram on the board is complete he asks the pupils to copy it down into their books. There follows a discussion about the names of co-ordinates. Again it is a discussion rather than a question and answer session; when one pupil offers a suggestion, he will ask another, 'Are you happy with that?' He very skilfully uses this process to develop the most efficient way of labelling and naming co-ordinates.

He then draws a line through a set of co-ordinates on the board and asks the group to work in pairs to put a name to this line. I think to myself, 'Well, they are just going to come up with something stupid like "Fred", or "Mary".' Indeed the first suggestion he gets back is of this type.

However, before I can say I told you so he gets another child at the board and asks them to draw the line 'Billy'. 'But that's silly,' they say, 'it could be anywhere.' This makes the point that the information needs to be detailed in order to exactly describe a line. There follows a ten-minute section during which pupils discuss and define the way you can describe a line so that the information is concise and only describes one possible line. At one stage a child describes this as 'being what maths is all about, giving a lot of information in an accurate and quick way'. By the end of this section we have got to a stage where the pupils are offering equations of lines like $y = x + 2$, $y = x$, $x = 4$, and so on. I never thought I would see the teaching of equations of lines made so interesting, and so relevant. When I talked to some of the pupils at a later date they remember this as their favourite maths lesson of the year.

Marc

All the people I admire have a command of their groups, and create a focus apparently effortlessly. They all teach well-prepared lessons in the sense that they fit into a wider context educationally, and everything within the lesson is tailored to drive that purpose. They think deeply about how they work, and constantly review what they do.

Tom put on an act in the classroom, some teachers do, some do not. I think for Tom this had been an effort at first, but it was something he now did without thinking. I remember being aware that whenever I was in his classroom, there was a calm and ordered atmosphere, that he was always talking to individual children, that everyone seemed to know what they were supposed to be doing, always. It was not as if he cracked jokes, or was loud, or physically dominated the room. He was a science teacher, and so the potential or disaster with equipment, flames and toxins was great, Tom, though, could introduce a lesson in which, say, 28 large and disruptive 15-year-olds would be released to do their worst, and yet they would listen to his apparently dry and very straightforward delivery, and would go on and do it, often very well. Why did they do this? They were groups which caused other teachers a lot of problems, Tom gave very clear instructions, and each child trusted him. By this I mean he had a very clear idea of what each child's learning needs were. People learn in many different ways, and within Tom's apparently straightforward presentation of a topic there were opportunities for everyone to do their best. Tasks were given out seemingly casually, 'Jim, would you go and work out the group's averages and put them on an OHP to save time?' Jim was thus both immobilised towards the end of a lesson when he had finished his experiment and might start being a problem, but also, for the only time in his day, others were relying on him. He was given responsibility. By the end of the first term that year,

Jim was succeeding across the whole curriculum because of the work that Tom had put in with him. It is probable that Tom was the only teacher who had approached Jim with the possibility of real success in mind. Tom knew all his pupils' strengths and weaknesses extremely well. He knew when to supply answers and when to demand them. He knew how to create the possibility of success.

All teachers work differently, and I think the vital thing to remember when watching others teach is that just because they do it differently to you, they still have something to offer. I always sneak, or it feels like I'm sneaking, a look at a particular colleague's blackboard when I'm passing through. It is a model of clarity and smart little visual ideas for letting even the poorest reader gain access to the contents of the writing. Another colleague seems able to engage a whole group in conversation. There's a lot of noise but it is all purposeful, and he draws out issues that I know I would have to approach differently, but the way he asks questions, the manner he has, somehow requires an opinion from the pupil he has questioned.

During my own teacher training Cliff taught groups of trainee teachers in a way which seemed to me to be exemplary. He managed to make everyone feel both safe and challenged. I remember his demonstration of evaporation and temperature involving his sudden appearance in a soaking T-shirt, and then the exposure of his scrawny upper torso, or him driving a discussion about conservation of energy by playing devil's advocate and creating imaginary machines before our eyes which defied everyone's definition. If he had said, 'We are going to discuss language use in physics, chemistry and biology today. Who'd like to start?' there would have been a long silence and many sighs. In the event, many people became more enthusiastic about science than they had been during their time studying the subject at university. In each case his huge knowledge base and his confidence in what he was doing enabled him to move one step ahead in any direction, whenever he needed to challenge anyone. I am not suggesting this is everyone's style, or that it is sustainable for term after school term, but the basic principles of preparation, high expectation and being a bit daft have certainly sustained me when I have feared teaching that terrible thing – the ordinary lesson. Everyone has them, by the way, its just that some people don't notice that they are doing it.

It is not just the good lessons that can help us. I can remember many lessons I have seen which could not be deemed successful. There are those that went spectacularly wrong and many which were less obviously unsuccessful. I can recall watching a science lesson in which none of the students were able to tell me what the connection was between the experiment they were doing and any previous or future work. The teacher was running this particular practical with a class for the first time without having already tried it out for himself. It was a relatively complicated experiment, and the teacher had become preoccupied with the difficulties it presented rather than the purpose for doing it. By the end of the lesson nothing had been achieved other than to put a generally well-motivated group in a bad mood through frustration, and of course, to make the most horrendous mess. Without the context for the experiment, the students were unable to make their own decisions and had taken every wrong turn possible.

I was reminded of this recently when I had to re-run a practical of my own. I had assumed I did not have to recap some fairly basic techniques before the group started work. In *my* mind they had done similar work not long ago. But I had forgotten what a small part of the pupils' day I formed – in their minds the previous sessions had disappeared into the mists of time. I introduced the second attempt with an admission that I had been wrong to expect them to succeed without a recap. This attempt went swimmingly (although there was still a mess!). I was reminded to always admit when I am wrong, or don't know the answer.

Dorothy

I used to work with someone called Jane who had trained as a secondary school teacher in the 1970s but who had mostly taught adults throughout her career. She taught me a lot and was an inspiration and a guide during the time we worked together.

Jane was always very precise about her work and took great care to research the needs and wants of her trainees, tailoring her training accordingly. She always planned ahead and tried to think of all eventualities using techniques such as sending questionnaires to potential trainees and adjusting the projected training as necessary to fit their needs. Her lesson plans were meticulously devised and broken down into realistically timed sections which allowed room for deviations and questions.

Jane had the ability to explain her subject (the financial aspects of business planning) with great ease and empathy. She taught from a very basic to an advanced level with the same easygoing but careful style. Her manner and attitude to her subject had the effect of making complex issues seem simple. She always took time to explain and never moved on until she was sure that the trainees understood what she was teaching. I observed her teaching individuals who had left school at 14 with no qualifications with the same ease as she taught those with Master's degrees.

Jane always took time to explain and by doing so she opened up her subject to many who would have otherwise rejected it. She gained a loyal following of successful business people who had been her trainees. She continued to work with many of her trainees for some years as she helped them through the development and growth of their businesses.

Jane's key strengths were that she:
- knew her subject;
- enjoyed teaching it;
- genuinely wanted others to learn;
- prepared meticulously;
- treated her trainees as equal;
- valued the experience they brought to the sessions;
- never patronised or made people feel foolish.

Another teacher who had a real impact on me was Tim. He taught me throughout the three years that I studied for my Institute of Personnel and Development (IPD) qualification. Tim was witty, irreverent and intensely knowledgeable with a seemingly devil-may-care attitude to teaching. He liked to laugh a lot and made his students laugh – he rarely seemed to take anything seriously but in reality he was passionately serious about many things, especially industrial relations which was his major subject.

Tim liked to illustrate his lessons with anecdotes, many of them drawn from real-life situations (his own and others'). His students, many of whom would have preferred that he stayed on the straight and narrow, did not always appreciate this. All of the IPD students were in full-time work and were studying through a combination of day release and their own time. Many students had had to fight for the time off work and some were self-financing. Others had won funding from their employers who expected to see a return on their money. It was often very difficult for the students to fit their studies into busy schedules and as a result they felt that every minute at college should be spent 'studying' in the traditional 'chalk and talk' sense of the word. They did not, in the main, enjoy discussions, role play or any non-traditional teaching methods, seeing them as a waste of precious time. They were very reluctant to discuss anything that was not in the textbooks or that did not seem to be directly relevant to the subject being taught. Their main concern was to pass the exams by swallowing the textbooks and regurgitating them as necessary. They did not see the relevance of the wider picture and felt that Tim's anecdotes, funny as they might be, had little or no bearing on the subject being taught.

Obviously, learning styles had a lot to do with this and perhaps it says something for the type of people who pass their exams and are successful in working as personnel officers! This experience of spending three years with fellow personnel students had a direct bearing on my decision not to follow this career path directly as I realised that I was not suited to work in the manner which seemed to be expected of personnel officers.

My learning style is highly visual and I seem to understand things better if I can see them in my mind. As a result I struggle with abstract concepts as I find it difficult to 'see' and therefore remember them. I was always very interested in Tim's stories as they provided a 'peg' for me to hang my learning on. The real-life stories gave the subject substance and relevance and also helped highlight the issues and dilemmas that I would need to be aware of when I became a practitioner myself.

I enjoyed Tim's lessons because they came alive with stories and humour and also because he would frequently draw a concept on the board when trying to explain it. This helped the visual side of my learning style to absorb and understand the information.

I enjoyed and emulate Tim's style because:
• he was knowledgeable about his subject;
• he used well-placed humour in his lessons;
• he handed control for learning to the student but gave copious support if needed;
• he taught in a 'visual' way which appealed to me;
• he widened the subject and put it into a real-life context.

My method of teaching is very similar to Tim's because I, too, like to tell anecdotes or use examples to get a point across. Stories tend to stick in people's minds and provide a useful trigger for remembering the learning at a later date.

I also tend to use illustrations to explain my subjects. If I'm trying to describe something verbally and sense that it is not being understood I will draw the concept or point. My drawings are pretty awful but they usually get the point across!

Another teacher who influenced me was Susan who taught on a computer course that I was also involved in. Susan was knowledgeable but seemed afraid of showing this. She was often unprepared for lessons, was easily distracted from the main subject, flapped and giggled a lot. She often said disarmingly frank but unwise things such as, 'I don't know why you have to learn this but you do and so I'll teach it to you.' The students would then proceed to switch off because she had sold the learning so badly that they could not see its relevance.

Susan thought her actions made her more of a friend to the students;

however this was not so. The students did not want a friend, they wanted a teacher who could help them through a complex subject. Most of the students did not respect Susan as she was unable to control the class and acted as if she was learning along with the students instead of leading them in their learning. The unfortunate aspect of this was that Susan was actually very intelligent but this was never made apparent to the students.

Jasbir

The time which I valued most in terms of my own development as a teacher was when I joined a high school near Leicester. I had just completed my probationary year and had recently got married and moved into the area. The school had only just opened and everything was brand new – the building, all the equipment and resources and, most importantly, the staff. We took in one year's intake and as a class teacher I moved with my class from subject to subject. The subject specialist would teach the lesson and the class teacher would support the pupils. so, although this school took pupils from 11–14 it had a thematic approach to the curriculum. As a staff we spent hours discussing the curriculum, building our team and talking about everything we did. As a new teacher it was a fabulous experience. I was able to work with and learn from experienced colleagues. The most important lessons they taught me were to constantly question what you do, and to remember that no matter who you are you have a voice.

As the only Asian teacher in the school I was seen as the font of knowledge of all Asian cultures. I had once again fallen into the trap of providing information about different festivals, cultures and anything else the other teachers quizzed me about. In this school the children who needed greatest support were Bengali children. This was the first time I had met any Bengal families and so I visited the libraries, built contacts in the community and found out how these families operated. This approach and the fact that I was valued by the school gave me the courage to say, 'I don't know the answer to your question but I do know how to find out.' An important lesson for all teachers to learn.

During this time I also became conscious of my Yorkshire accent and issues of dialect. The teachers at this school recognised the importance of dialect. In assisting the children to understand and operate in Standard English, which is in effect the dialect of school, they avoided making them feel excluded by the language they brought with them, and which they reverted to outside class. They taught me that a language difference is not a language deficiency. The child who speaks a language or dialect other than Standard English has much to offer both teachers and peers.

Another lesson I have carried with me from this school was how to value the achievements of all children. On a Friday afternoon we had a Special Mentions Assembly. Each teacher would mention certain children who had done something special during the week. The achievements were not just academic achievements and ranged from acts of kindness to winning competitions. I have continued with this approach in the school I work in today: we not only have a Special Mentions Assembly but also a Special Mentions Board in the entrance hall and Special Mentions Books in every classroom. Special mentions can come from teachers, parents, support staff and other children.

Vicky

I have worked with Matthew in science and film-based workshops on numerous occasions. I particularly remember one occasion in Hatfield Galleria Shopping Centre. We were running a DNA film workshop as part of a public understanding of science fair. We likened the medium of film to DNA and people drew directly onto the frames of film to represent genes – the result was a projected animated film. What particularly struck me about the way Matthew worked was the time he gave individuals to ask questions. He always seemed to have time to listen and then to explain. By attracting everyone's attention at the very beginning he gave them all a chance to understand what the session was going to be about, get them thinking and talking. People were delighted to have their own questions valued, and properly and intelligently answered by a 'scientist' who spoke using clear language about a subject it was obvious he was very knowledgeable and enthusiastic about.

I also respect the way that Matthew treats his students. One reason I always felt I could not be a classroom teacher was to do with behaviour and discipline problems with children. Matthew seems to take these in his stride. He is totally straight with his students and expects them to behave. If someone is disrupting others he will make sure they know he knows. He will get through to this person by being persistent, not by shouting and being a tyrant. By not putting up with any trouble he has gained a real relationship with many students.

Roger and Gerry are two workshop leaders I have worked with who have very different styles, and work with very different subject matter, yet always appear absolutely in command of their sessions and are clearly dedicated to their work as well as enjoying it.

Gerry runs drama groups for adults with various disabilities. I have learnt from her that the key is to find the inspirational situation for a particular group to work in. The clearest examples that come to mind feature celebrations. In one she became a Christmas tree demanding decoration. 'Who is going to put my lights on?'. 'How can you have finished? I haven't got a fairy on top yet' and so on. Her demands required that the whole group thought about and responded to her actions. Similarly at Easter she became the 'noisy one' on the production line making hot cross buns – 'Ooh, isn't it hot in here – bring us a cup of tea, love' – leading to amusement but more importantly the involvement of all. In this way she shows her groups that she expects them to be involved; she seems to exude a confidence that they will succeed in anything they attempt. She dares to be different, has put on performances in which people with profound disabilities dance with able-bodied professionals. Although this can seem shocking at first it both challenges preconceptions and is evidence of her high expectations in practice. Her methods both entertain her students and motivate them – I realised early on how much she moves amongst her students and from that day on made sure I moved amongst the groups I was working with, more than I think I was doing previously.

Roger organises and runs film workshops. Working with Roger always reminds me that it is all right to take your time, to speak slowly when explaining something and, most importantly, when not to speak. He seems to make things happen with a minimum of fuss, flap and noise – even though there is usually a group of children, cameras, projectors, video equipment and bits and pieces for making things all precariously balanced in the space. Screens and lights are all strewn across a borrowed room. When I work with Roger I am not only aware that he knows what he is talking about but I feel re-inspired through his dedication and inspirational ideas to carry on doing what I do.

So, you might say, he speaks slowly and often doesn't talk at all, she is bubbly and enthusiastic and constantly commentating. What am I supposed to do, which style is best? Obviously I don't want to copy one person exactly. What I do draw from these three very different teachers is the different ways that they develop a creative atmosphere: they all have high expectations, they know what they are talking about and can convince others of their knowledge. They also all have the patience to take their time if they want to communicate a particular piece of information. I like to think I draw on elements of all three of these teachers in my own work, and adapt their styles into my own.

Helen

Frances and I taught together on many occasions. We have team-taught groups in drama, young people training to become effective school councillors, and students teachers on a PGCE course. The day we trained the student councillors showed Frances at her best and gave me much to think about for my own practice.

The student councillors we were working with had been elected by their form groups, and the aim of the training was to build a team which could use the limited school council meeting time in school most effectively. Frances and I shared leading the activities although we had jointly planned them. This gave me time and space to observe and reflect on Frances's teaching style as well as the reactions of the students within the group. Frances's explanations were concise, her tone of voice non-patronising and intelligent, and clear eye contact was made with all students.

During the last part of the day Frances observed a mock student council meeting, during which the issues surrounding their elections as student counsellors were shared and discussed. One of the students chaired this mock meeting, which was the first time a student had taken on the responsibility for running any part of the day. The group engaged in a lively game of 'pretend'. Frances fed back her observations at the end of the session. She described how most of the active participants during the 'mock meeting' had found it difficult not to refer to me for access to the debate, even though my role had been to record on flipcharts the main points of the discussion. In this way she gently pointed out our aim of giving the pupils autonomy in these meetings. She also explained to others that they had opted out of the session for the first time during the day. This made the point that for meetings to be effective all students had to be prepared to be involved.

Frances's feedback held the attention of the whole group in an extraordinary way. I think each student was eager to hear whether her interpretations and observations of them were fair, interesting and authentic, and from the nods and murmurs of agreement, there was a sense of satisfaction at a job well done pervading the room at the end. No one had been picked out in an negative sense, but each manifestation of inappropriate behaviour was reflected on to maximise learning.

For me, 'Watching Others Work' means this kind of team planning – teaching and evaluation of either a single lesson, or at its best a series of related lessons. The learning opportunities are multiplied for myself and my students. I actively seek support for students in the classroom from colleagues and friends who have some valuable experience or knowledge to offer. I have had to build confidence in myself to get to this stage to feel 'good enough' about myself as a teacher and a person.

I read the term 'good enough' with relief in an article about parenting when I was being made to feel like an inadequate parent by some friends. I returned to work when my child was three months old, and they were overstressing how difficult it all must be, checking I wasn't worried about the detrimental effect this would have on the child's development. In this context for me 'good enough' doesn't mean 'second rate' – it means that all children deserve the best you can *realistically* manage, whether you are teaching a lesson or interacting more informally with a pupil. If we have false hopes and expectations and imitate teaching styles which don't suit us, we may only succeed in mirroring rather than complementing another teacher's style. I remember clearly as a beginning teacher the pressure I was under to become like my head of department, being trained up for 'their' department. Now I believe observed teaching is most valuable when it is unconsciously affecting another teacher's style.

I know that I need to be inspired by what I am teaching, and excited about the possible outcomes. This makes me inspirational at the planning stages and my liveliness spills over into the classroom. The closing remarks in an observation of a lesson by a recent head read, 'Helen is clearly a teacher who enjoys being with and teaching her students.' The down side of this is that I can become too fixed on the 'bright' ideas and what I think the outcomes should be, and in practice a little over-enthusiastic in achieving them at the expense of picking up important points which need clarifying.

Each time I have taught with Frances I have noticed that we share a determination and enthusiasm to allow the students to succeed. Listening to her planning and teaching has made me realise she has the ability to ask me or the students a considered and reflective question which inevitably deepens the learning and checks understanding. She models a way of reinforcing the lesson expectations which is non-threatening, and challenges inappropriate behaviour by making everyone in the group accept responsibility for themselves. The sessions are therefore not always comfortable, but learning often comes out of these challenges.

Colleagues who have most influenced me are 'real people' with the students. There is an authenticity in all their communications with young people. These are not the charismatic 'actor' teachers who absorb and entrain. I have learnt from such teachers, but usually feel overawed by the cult of the personality rather than excited by the learning opportunities. There is a different kind intensity, a precision and focus in the best teachers' use of language and intention, and a mutual respect between teacher and student. The most influential teachers can create a moment of intensity when a student is struggling with an answer which becomes critical for them. They are supported in these significant moments by teachers who are learning themselves, listening intently and responding as if that issue is all that matters to everyone in the room.

Reflection

Looking back over the stories in this section the initial focus is on the teachers. What a wonderful collection. You may wish you had been taught by some or all of them. It is also important to consider the individual scribes of these memories. What makes them tick? What makes them see these different qualities as strengths? What makes these qualities *register*, remain, endure and become absorbed into their own styles. Place yourself back in the classroom again, captivated by a particular person within a particular subject. For that moment, maybe for that whole lesson, you are hooked, you understand, *you are learning*. Now shift to thinking about the teacher, who they are, not necessarily as a person in their own right, but what motivates their wish to pass their subject on to you?

We have all stressed the importance of the relationship between the teacher and the learner; we all acknowledge the need for an unfussy, non-patronising approach. A respectful knowledge of your class as individuals with unique strengths and weaknesses would also seem to be essential. Gauging when to be relaxed and approachable, balanced with the ability to be quietly assertive at any given moment also seems vital, either as a point of discipline or even to provide your learners with the reassuring knowledge that a learned perspective is there to be called on during times of debate and explanation.

A detailed knowledge of your subject area, good preparation, thoughtful lesson structure and skilled use of appropriate language are all elements which seem to make up good lessons too, although perhaps what shines through is the ability to bring style, enthusiasm and character into lessons in a natural, non-domineering fashion.

Most of all, what you should have drawn from these experiences is never, never to underestimate your class. The giving of responsibility, the ability to see pupils as novice artists, mathematicians, chemists, the value of all the class members' experiences and perspectives all help learners develop a sense of ownership and participation in their own education, and allow them to value the time spent with their classmates, and you – their teacher.

Questions for your journal

You have read descriptions of the colleagues that have influenced us most. You may not have had the luxury of working alongside expert teachers yet but the following questions may help you start to think about what you will draw on when you do.

- Which of these descriptions most closely describes a lesson you would want to teach?
- What is it in the description you most value?
- List the common qualities that the teachers described here possess.
- Can you pick out from this list three key qualities a good teacher must have?
- Can you remember a time when you were made responsible for a part of your own learning? How did you feel about it at the time? How do you feel about it now?
- Can you remember a time when you surprised yourself by managing to do something you didn't know you could do?

Chapter 7

Our Best Lessons

Introduction

Our own best lessons don't come out of thin air. Nothing we do is original. Teachers should not feel as though they have to be original. Of course even teachers who appear original aren't, they have just learnt how to take good ideas either from others or from books and adapt them so that they become a part of their own individual style. Their skill is to have in their heads a wide range of possible approaches to working with pupils. Their craft is to use the right style at the right time.

There is much talk at present about school effectiveness and school improvement. Much of this is based around the need for strong management. Clearly a good head teacher will make our life easier but this chapter is about what individual teachers and groups of teachers can do in their own classrooms. Individual teachers can make a difference, you have got choices about how you want to work. The lessons described here will hopefully help you make the choices which feel right for you.

Marc

"I often find it useful to compare two lessons that have something in common. It might be their content, style of delivery, something about the group, even where it was taught. The lessons described here were both successful, one more so than the other, and both involved students who were being difficult to teach. What is unusual about the two lessons is that one was an academically weak group of GCSE students, mostly boys, faced with the prospect of learning about chemical equations on the morning of the last day of term before the Christmas holidays, and the other was a group of adults who were at their class voluntarily, had paid for the privilege, and who took me completely by surprise.

There are several ways to gain control of a difficult class, and they fall into two categories: those which work for that day only, and those which attempt to address the reasons for the poor behaviour and hence improve learning in the long-term. The second method requires little more than that you establish a reputation for being someone who always follows up incidents, always contact parents, always makes sure that whatever the stated sanction was, happens. This takes time, but is worth it. You will find it prevents a lot of arguments later. Recently I had five students in detention who would all have needed chasing up when I first started in the school. They all appeared on time, uncomplaining, and a fresh start was established. With the groups below I used a mixture of short- and long-term persuasion.

The pre-Christmas class was tricky. I had recently taken over from another teacher, and the students had low expectations of themselves. I started at ten o'clock on the Friday morning of the last day of the Christmas term to teach them chemical equations. They were horrified on two counts; firstly that they were being expected to work, and secondly that I thought they would be able to do chemical equations.

An hour later the least literate, generally most unco-operative student with the lowest self-regard (and hence an inversely large amount of associated disruption) was standing at the front of the class, holding the chalk, waving his arms around and saying firmly to another student, 'No, look at it again, Gemma. Count the carbons. It's got two, see? And four hydrogens.' Then swiftly over his shoulder to me, 'That's right, eh, Sir?'

How did we move from Yuletide indifference to a heated debate about hydrocarbons? The first trick was both to expect plenty, and to offer a challenge. The second was to let the pupils see that what I was expecting was both fair and possible. Many disruptive pupils do not engage because they think the rules of the game are constructed to exclude them. Much of their experience tells them this. So, to start the lesson I said, 'Merry Christmas. By 11 o'clock I'll bet you're doing these,' (indicating a complicated-looking equation on the board). 'These are particularly easy for people who don't read too well, because no one in your year has heard of this stuff and so you're all starting from the same spot. Can anyone here not count to five?' Silence. 'Good, because that may have caused a problem. You have to be able to count to five to do these.'

Gauntlet thrown, looks of 'can he be serious?' But, above all else, focus. I broke down what seemed like an impenetrable job into steps; I did not talk down to the students, and they were not quite sure what to expect next. To keep the focus, I had all the students around the front desk and dished out jobs. 'You be carbon, you be iron', and so on. The students enacted a chemical reaction, and all the while I referred to the equations on the board beside us. By the time the reaction was complete, bonds (chemical ones) broken and remade, most students were using the symbolic names for chemicals, and understood the conventions relating to the numbers in the equations, simply by trying to use them. I was clearly, as they saw it, taking a risk with this group. They spent a lot of time in school being given easy work, not being allowed out of their seats, and rarely saw anything that they had not already failed at, often more than once.

I ended up with a small controlled explosion, wrote the reactant on the board and asked for suggestions as to what had caused the explosion. They gave full and thoughtful answers.

It is easy in activities like this to lose individuals, and for the keenest or loudest pupils to dominate. We must not ignore those who learn by watching alone whilst we must check that everyone processes the information. In the lesson I directed questions at individuals by name rather than asking questions of the whole class. As a team spirit had been proposed - you'll be doing these by 11 – there was a pressure to listen in case you were asked and slowed in process up by not having listened. That Christmas I like to think they talked of nothing else but how they balanced a tricky chemcial equation.

My naughty adults caught me off guard. This can happen at any time. A group which has never previously given problems, or reportedly docile new group, can suddenly become hard to manage. It is important to have a response ready, because a steamroller approach early on can result in the expectation that you will always be heavy handed and behaviour will rise to meet the challenge. This particular session was a tutorial for adults who had paid to be there. I was talking to the group, about ten minutes into the session, in a lovely comfortable old room, and I suddenly realised that there were levels of background conversation going on which I would never allow in my school classroom while I or another student was talking to the group. With this group I used short-term measures: I was only going to meet them on another couple of occasions anyway. I found myself thinking what would I do in school? I spent the rest of the session moving around the room, using individual names to punctuate sentences, 'and so, Jean, these elements tend to group together because . . .?' or physically standing behind someone who was being noisy. Firstly, they then can't hear themselves, and neither can they see you. Also, their own audience is looking at you as well as them. They have to choose who to listen to. Since you are supposed to be in charge they look at you. I even gave out a little busy work to the worst offender: 'I've not got the right form with me. Can you jot everyone's names down whilst I introduce this?' Neutralised, wrongfooted and failing to annoy me, visibly at least, Mr Noisy managed to learn more than he had set out to at the start of the evening.

I remember that in my first year of teaching I was given some advice by a colleague nearing retirement. 'You'll get very tired,' he said. 'So don't be afraid to come in, give them some writing for the whole lesson, and when they've gone chuck it in the bin. It'll give you a breather.' While I do not for a second endorse this advice, I endorse the message that you cannot teach spectacular lessons the whole time. You will be tired, you will be in a hurry, your mind will be on other things. But it is worth pausing when you know something special has just happened. Try to work out why it went so well – in that way you are more likely to be able to repeat it.

Dorothy

I once worked as an area co-ordinator for a national women's training organisation which ran programmes on a regional basis. Each area co-ordinator was responsible for designing their course, recruiting participants, recruiting trainers and teaching some of the course themselves. The ultimate aim was to train women to run their own businesses.

I loved the job as my employers gave me free reign to run the course as I saw fit. I recruited mainly through advertising in the press, posters and word of mouth. I sent information packs through the post and told the course participants I would introduce myself to them on enrolment.

I got off to a bad start when a woman called Lynn, who, on entering the training room, walked straight past my outstretched hand and shook hands with my white colleague, assuming she was the course leader. Her face fell when she realised that the young black woman in front of her was actually the course leader. This was to mark the beginning of a difficult relationship with Lynn.

Around half the women on the course were older than me yet they accepted my role without hesitation. However, it seemed that Lynn tried at all times to undermine my authority and confidence. Her constant jibes about my age and her *sotto voce* racist comments were an irritant and a distraction which I tried to ignore rather than give her the attention and confrontation that she sought. Her strategy paid off one day, two weeks into the course, when she made a racist comment which I could not ignore.

I stopped the session and asked Lynn why she felt able to make such a comment. Could she not see that her behaviour was racist? She shrugged and replied, 'Perhaps it is – so what? Black people don't belong in England so if you come here you should expect abuse.' I wondered what had led her to this conclusion. She told me that I had come to the country uninvited. I reminded her of the fact that the British Government had in fact sent out urgent calls to the colonies begging for an influx of labour. In fact this had been co-ordinated by Enoch Powell. Our argument flowed backwards and forwards, with me responding to every accusation she threw at me.

Suddenly the whole class was sitting up and listening. I had previously tried to keep personal feelings and politics out of what was essentially a business course but this was abandoned over the next two hours as the discussion raged heatedly over racism, colonialism, sexism, homophobia, disability, class and many other topics. People who had rarely spoken before became very animated and those who had previously held the floor in discussions were forced to listen to the views of others. People with fixed ideas were asked to justify their views and found themselves in the position of having to explain feelings and beliefs they had taken for granted.

The end of the lesson came but students ignored this and carried on with the discussion. We continued through tea break and through the next session until we were forced to leave by the arrival of another group in the room. Even so, the debate continued in the canteen and in small groups elsewhere around the building.

This was a turning point in the course. Many of the women approached me individually or in groups to thank me for allowing them the time and space to discuss these issues. Some of them had never before thought through the issues which had been raised and had been shocked by their own attitudes and beliefs. These attitudes had been preventing the group from working together effectively as unspoken tensions existed between the different women, from different backgrounds, who made up the course. Obviously some problems remained, and there were no overnight conversions. The group agreed among themselves to a set of ground rules covering issues of trust, respect and equality and also agreed to follow them for the rest of the course.

The group now had a basis from which to constructively criticise and this allowed them to deal with difficult situations, such as racist comments, in a different way. They now had the mutually agreed ground rules to back them up. The sessions would often be brought to an unscheduled halt so that we could discuss a comment or situation that had arisen, but thanks to the ground rules and the in-depth discussion which led to their creation, it was never necessary to spend more than a few minutes on these discussions.

At first I worried that these interruptions were taking us away from the main element but the students were adamant that for them this was an essential part of the process. They did not want to lose it. They felt a greater ownership of the course and felt that these discussions lent substance to their learning. In fact at the end of course review many of them cited this as one of the most positive aspects of the course and their only complaint was that they wished we had had more time in which to delve into these subjects.

I think I have remembered this as one of the most positive sessions I have taught as I learnt that:
- it is not always necessary or advisable to stick to a lesson plan if situations arise which need dealing with instantly;
- it is not always possible to separate personal issues from academic issues, in fact keeping the two apart can hinder learning;
- students learn better if they feel committed to their own learning and have a sense of ownership over the course.

Another lesson I remember as a success was as a student teacher of English as a Foreign Language. I was delivering an observed lesson, and was nervous as I was working with a group who had always appeared passive and uninterested when I had seen them previously. The group consisted of graduates from all over the world seeking to improve their English before embarking on postgraduate studies in English universities.

My tutor had asked me to deliver the lesson on the theme of 'hunger' but left it to me to plan and decide on the resources I would use. I chose to explore world hunger and famine and arrived armed with maps and charts showing the distribution of major food-producing countries and food consumers. I brought a publication showing the situations caused by famine and shopped at local stores for millet, cornmeal, couscous, plantains, green bananas and other tropical foodstuffs. Finally I bought my 'red nose' as it was a few weeks before the annual Red Nose charity day.

I began by asking the class to define hunger using as many English words as they could. We then looked at the maps and they were asked to explain why it is that 800 million people within the agriculturally rich 'Third World' live under threat of famine rather than we, the consumers of the food they produce. At this point I glanced across at my supervisor's notes. She had written, 'Dorothy has pitched the level too high for these students.' I was somewhat discouraged but carried on regardless. However, having seen her notes and remembering my past experience of this group I was expecting the lesson to be a struggle.

To my surprise the group came alive. I was faced by a sea of waving hands as they all clamoured to speak; it seemed every student had a theory which they wanted to share. We had an analysis of hunger and poverty from various political, social and economic perspectives. They reasoned and argued animatedly with each other and I observed students who usually spent their time doodling on their writing pads fighting for space to put their argument forward.

I then produced the food I had purchased and arranged it on the table in front of me. Suddenly the tone of the lesson changed again as people literally gasped with delight as each item emerged from the shopping bag. They explained that they had been in England for many months, living in halls of residence or as lodgers. They were fed a mainly English diet and missed their foods from home. They quizzed me as to where I had bought such goods and how much it cost and I worked these questions and answers into the lesson. The group passed the foods around and explained what the foods were called in their language, and how they prepared and served them. They discovered that many dishes were prepared in similar ways in different countries and also learnt new ways to cook familiar ingredients.

To end the lesson I ducked under the desk and emerged with my red nose in place. When the laughter subsided we debated whether the Red Nose appeal was an appropriate response to hunger and famine. Their answer was a resounding 'No', and they proceeded to debate the reasons why. The students were in full flow when the bell went to signal the end of the lesson. They crowded round the table to talk to me and to look at the foodstuffs and only reluctantly left for their lunch break when prompted by my tutor who needed space to discuss the lesson with me.

She said I had done well and that she had never seen the group so animated. However, she would deduct marks as I had failed to contain the lesson within the time allowed, and I had strayed from the subject. She did not mention the note I had seen about the level being too high for these students. On leaving the classroom I was met by almost the whole group who had waited for me. One of them, a good English speaker said, 'I have been asked by the others to tell you that was the most interesting and informative lesson we had had since starting at this college.' He explained that the reason they normally appeared so disinterested was that they felt the lessons insulted their intelligence. Normally a lesson in 'hunger' would have covered sentences such as 'John is hungry', 'Susan is also hungry', 'My hunger caused me to faint', and so on. They felt this was way below their level and they were tired of the ritualistic sentence construction which seemed, to them, to epitomise learning English.

They had welcomed the chance to practise their English-speaking skills by reasoning and debating as they felt these skills were more appropriate for their postgraduate studies. They were overwhelming in their praise and I floated home on a cloud of happiness.

I had observed my supervising teacher in action with this group and had admired her skills. Yet I had managed to get through to the students in a way that she had never done. This gave me an immense feeling of satisfaction and boosted my confidence. Two years later I met one of the students who told me that my lesson was the only one he could remember from the year-long course and that it had made a lasting impression on him.

This lesson demonstrated, for me, the importance of pitching lessons at the right level, so as to challenge and stimulate the desire to learn. I try never to underestimate the abilities of groups I work with. It was also a boost as a novice teacher to realise that the old tried and tested methods are not always relevant and that there are may ways of enabling students to learn.

Helen

The hall was transformed by basic theatre lighting into an oval performance space with two rows of seating forming the perimeter. Each of the 80 participants knew their own roles and all the songs, but none of them or the staff had knowledge of how the whole would fit together into a performance.

The students were performers and audience, and the staff each had an area of expertise which had contributed to the whole – songs rehearsed, sculptures made and lines learnt from a script which had been devised around the theme of space travel from the school yard.

The countdown began over the microphone, and as if by magic the 80 voices sang the 'MGB Lifts Off' anthem, accompanied by a variety of student musicians able to perform at their own level of competence. Immediate fade into the first piece of backing tape and that was the only cue the 'All Mod Cons' team of school cleaners needed as they entered the performance space. The initial nervousness and unfamiliarity soon became the challenge each character had needed to lift their performance out of the ordinary. Reputations were at stake – ours is not an easy school to be seen as 'uncool' (is any school?). I shared keenly how each student felt as this was the first attempt I'd made at my new school to provide a whole year group with a shared experience, and I was doing it in front of my colleagues. Past experience reassured me that the students would accept the challenge, but they are far more resilient than the experienced teacher!

There were some highs and lows during the morning's activities, not least the staff who couldn't handle the apparent spontaneous creativity of the events – a performance that was neither polished nor for an audience other than the participants, of which the adults were a part and parcel.

These teachers were not used to feel 'out of control' in this way. The discipline was coming from the outline script posted around the room on huge flipcharts as well as the most active performers who were anxious to see what their weeks of work could become. The staff who had faith in the students' interest and ability knew that the learning outcomes were as predictable as helping a child towards literacy, and were inspired to become better teachers in an intensive learning course rarely experienced in these days of the over-prescribed National Curriculum. The morning culminated in the 'surprise' arrival of an alien during the last song, who was offered the strangely beautiful and colourful 3D sculptures. Visiting staff from other curriculum areas were struck by the impressive 'suspension of disbelief' as each pair of students admired their creation as the creature from another planet arranged them in the magically lit performance space.

My pride at the student's capability had been matched at the end of my first term, when I had encouraged the students and staff to put on a variety-style concert which celebrated the diverse cultures in the school. The link throughout the evening was the co-hosting by an English-speaking drag artist from one of the show pieces of the event, and the serene Urdu teacher in stunning Salwa Kameese. The comperes introduced the acts alternately and watched each other as they spoke. The initial murmurings in the audience about what was going on were quickly replaced by a thoughtful acceptance that some of the audience and performers were clearly 'getting the jokes' in Urdu.

The head commented that this single demonstration of 'equal but different' had increased the status of many students' home language amongst themselves and those who were unluckily monolingual. The Year 10 students who are organising the Asian Fashion Event in the spring have quite naturally adopted the two-hander style of compering. The 'business plan' of the event handed in to the Senior Managers and Parents' Association included this as a reason why they should allow the event to happen.

I mention more than my initial 'best lesson' plan in order to make several points about the sheer scale of exciting work possible in the primary and secondary school. Taking the best of the students' experiences and abilities in any subject area can lead to what will become their most memorable lessons in school, whether strictly speaking 'lessons' at all. The only pre-requisites are:

- Knowing what role you are best at in a team-teaching situation – do you initiate, complete, organise or reflect? Or could you become the sort of teacher who can provide stimulating lead sessions for a massed 'audience'?

- Knowing your students well enough for there to be mutual trust – you expect a great deal from them, but they know without a shadow of a doubt that you will not let them fail.
- Giving students the chance to surprise you and not over-organising every minute of every experience on offer in your subject area – learning with and from your students and colleagues.

My driving force is how to achieve this level of commitment in young people whose lives impinge on their learning time, and amongst colleagues who have 'seen the film, read the book'. I learn from watching others work in its broadest sense, including the students. My ambition is to teach at my best with humour and sensitivity after an ex-Year 11 student told me I was doing fine, but I'd do better if I was to 'lighten up a bit'. I had achieved intensity without reassurance, commitment with blinkers and he knew what was wrong instinctively. I have only ever been unhappy in a working environment which discouraged this level of communication with the students, and where the students were criticised for not thinking for themselves. All young people think for themselves. It is a privilege if they will share their thoughts with you, and the best teachers know how to create the climate necessary for this.

Vicky

It was a lively group of nine adults with learning disabilities. I was showing them how the dramatic use of camera angles can enhance a story and I made up an exercise I call Video Consequences. Each shot had to be taken from a different angle and we would build up a story as a result of the last shot. It was important that we completed this within one hour, that everyone was involved, and that there was time to watch the video at the end. We could all see the image on the monitor. We had one photoflood light, a camera and a tripod.

I put the camera high up at first and asked someone to look at it from the floor. She saw herself on the monitor, saw what it was all about and immediately yelled 'Help' and clasped her hands in dramatic distress. The next shot had the camera on the floor looking up with another member of the group looking down sternly into it. This continued – we had the camera crooked on the floor so that the floor looked like a hill with someone climbing up it, we used shadows for a fight, close-ups of scared and smiling faces. Finally, I dubbed some silent movie piano music over it.

Why was this successful? Because:
- we discovered a way of telling a story;
- the group inadvertently learnt to use the camera creatively;
- the group understood how the ideas could be used again;

- everyone was involved;
- we were working together and listening to each other;
- it was seemingly spontaneous although there was a clear structure;
- the result was satisfying;
- a lively working atmosphere was created;
- everyone enjoyed it;
- I felt uplifted and invigorated at the end, felt we had moved on and something had been learnt.

Another video workshop that always works is using a stop-frame technique or substitution trick. You stop the camera running without altering its position, but you change the position of the people or do a substitution before starting the camera running again. So the person vanishes into thin air, or the person who was about to fall down stairs is substituted by a model. By working through this fairly simple technique, everyone gains an understanding of how the trick is done and yet the result is fresh.

As an introduction to film and animation I like to run an instant film workshop. This involves drawing directly onto 16mm film and projecting it as big as possible. I have done this with all ages and abilities. It is versatile because it works at different levels; you can work frame by frame or make any mark on the film to get an interesting result which is never quite what you expect.

Both these ideas:
- help demystify an aspect of the subject;
- catch the students' attention;
- let them play with the idea and work on it in their own way;
- have pleasing overall results and transform the practical work into something special;
- have the potential to lead on to other projects.

Debbion

I have just directed a piece for a new works festival in Leicester. The piece involved six black women. There was one key session which formed the blueprint for the whole piece. I knew that if they did not like this session they would leave. It was an experiential process – I went in with guidelines which I shared with the group. I was clear about the process I wanted us all to follow but the outcome was left open. During this session we explored ways in which we could tell our own stories through the use of voice, movement and poetry. We spent time acknowledging each person's story, finding similarities and differences and drawing on all of this to create an exciting performance. The group had taken a collective responsibility for the end product, this only succeeded as each individual had contributed and felt that their contribution was valued by others. Everyone had also supported other members of the group in their contributions.

Another success was not a lesson as such but an example of how changes in institutional habits can contribute to learning and education in the broadest sense. In the student union common room at an FE college for 16–19-year-olds we introduced monthly and weekly current teenage magazines. This encouraged a change in the sorts of discussion which took place in the common room. It also encouraged the students to interact much more than they had been doing. Boys read the problem pages in the girl's magazines, began asking questions about sex and talking far more openly than they had been used to. This helped dispel a lot of myths they still carried around with them. This was also the time of a general election, and many students had no concept of change and were nervous of any change – I realised that there was no point lecturing them on political issues, I had to be ready to listen to their fears and help them talk through issues for themselves if they were to reach decisions which made sense to them.

Another session I remember fondly is one in which I asked all members of the group I was working with to make their own 'altars'. I brought in objects such as postcards, sand, candles and each member of the group constructed their own altar space. We visited each other's space and told our own stories explaining what each thing symbolised. I think this worked so well because no one could get it wrong. Everyone's story was the right one, and important for each individual.

Tony

I want to explore what makes a 'good' lesson, from both my point of view and from pupils' points of view. I recently asked the group of 10–11-year-olds I am working with to think back over the last two terms and describe the best maths session we have had together. They remembered two sessions in particular; one session in which we had explored the relationship between the distance around our heads and our height, where we ended up with a huge scatter gram on the wall with all our initials on it and various 'lines of best fit;' to explore the ratio. The other session they particularly remembered was one during which we worked together on visualising multilink cubes, making mental images of different arrangements and then attempting to describe these arrangements from different viewpoints. I asked the pupils to jot notes down in their journals to explain to me why these were good lessons. These were the responses from the 56 pupils:

- the sessions were fun/interesting (12);
- we worked with our friends, helped each other and learnt from each other (10);
- we learnt something we didn't already know (10);
- they were practical, we could use equipment and the computers (8);
- the sessions were hard and challenging (6);
- the teacher explained things well (6);
- the lessons were easy (3);
- we did all different sorts of maths in these lessons (1).

These responses immediately raised questions in my mind: as the reason given by most pupils was to do with interest and fun, does this mean that most of my lessons are dull and uninteresting, or do the reasons that follow suggest what makes a lessons interesting and fun? The group clearly place a high value on working with each other and see the importance of learning from each other as well as from a teacher 'who explains it well'. Do I give enough opportunities for this particularly in my mathematics sessions? I clearly still do not incorporate IT and equipment sufficiently as these responses suggest that the novelty remains. Perhaps the most interesting were the responses of two groups of pupils: one of whom enjoyed the sessions because they had found them challenging, and the other who enjoyed it because it was easy. I take this as a pointer of success for the differentiation of activities. The group who found it hard, challenging, yet enjoyable were those pupils who on the whole can 'do' the maths I ask them to look at. They are clearly confident enough to push themselves and be pushed by me to explore quite complex mathematics. The three pupils who suggested that the activities were easy are those who on the whole find maths 'hard' and a bit of a struggle. Their response suggests to me that they found a certain security within these activities. I guess my aim may be to get these three to a stage where they too can enjoy challenge and difficulty without it affecting their mathematical confidence.

I also enquired of the group what would have made the lessons 'better'. They could only come up with two reasons: more time would have been appreciated, and some of the pupils who enjoy pushing on so they feel in front of everyone else suggested that they could have worked individually as well as in groups. It's a fair cop, I thought.

Let me explain the session in more detail. The *How far around my head* session was used as an introduction to a half-term's topic entitled 'true or false'. I wanted to introduce the idea of hypothesis testing. So, I had all the Year 6 pupils in a middle space between their two classrooms. I asked, 'If I was to measure around our head, how many times would I be able to fit that length into your height.' 'Loads' and 'What do you mean?' came the responses.

'Well, do you think your height will be three times the distance around your head?' I continued.

'No – more,' suggested someone.

'What, four?,' said I.

So, we took a vote and the answers ranged from two to five. I put up a large piece of squared paper on the wall with two axes marked 'height' and 'distance around head'. Everyone in the class took their measurements and marked them on the squared paper in the form of a scatter graph. I also asked everyone to label their 'point' with their initials, and asked, girls to use one colour for their cross, boys to use another colour and any adults who could be persuaded to take part to use a third colour.

Over lunchtime I drew on a line of best fit – it worked out at about 2.5 × distance round head = height. We then all got back together and talked about what we had discovered. More importantly individuals in the group noticed things like a cluster for the adults, and girls and boys appearing in groups. 'Is it different for boys and girls and adults?' they asked. This led neatly into a discussion about testing hypotheses often leading on to more questions rather than simply answering a problem.

The moment that stays with me is two boys suddenly shouting at each other in the middle space. I went over and asked what the problem was. One boy was irate – 'He's put his cross in the wrong place,' he said. 'Look, it can't be there, I'm taller than him and it's further along than mine.' It was the first – and last time – I saw this particular pupil take this much care over interpreting data on a graph!

I suppose the *Multilink models* session would be described as 'whole-class teaching'. Again, I was at the front between the two classrooms, this time holding a piece of multilink in my hand. I said, 'I want you all to close your eyes.' I was surprised how readily they did this and I was faced with 64 pairs of eyes closed and silence.

Now, make a multilink cube appear in your mind – it can be any colour ... 'Can you all see one?' Silent nods; frowns of concentration.

'Now, move it around so that you can see the little lump on top ... Have you all done that?' More nods.

'Now, make another one appear, move it all around the first one, then stick the two together. Move your two multilinks around so that you look at them from all sides.'

We repeated this process until all the group claimed to have visualised 3-D shapes constructed from multilink. I asked the group to remember what shape they had made and open their eyes. Individuals then drew representations of their shapes on the board until we had drawn all the different shapes visualised by the group. We then explored how to draw plan views and views from the sides. The group then moved away and worked on activities linked to 3D representations on isometric paper and plan views and side elevations.

What is particularly fascinating for me about this session is that I cannot carry out the tasks I had asked the pupils to do. I told them at the end – they all assured me that they could do it. Maybe one day someone will teach me how to visualise.

Jasbir

The best thing that I can think of from my time in school is becoming a headteacher. I never envisaged being a headteacher: even when I qualified as a teacher, being a head never entered my mind. I don't really know why. Perhaps because I enjoyed being with children so much I wanted to teach, not push paper around. I also thought that if I became a headteacher I might become unpopular and I didn't like being unpopular. Maybe deep down I also thought that people like me don't become headteachers.

When the head at the school at which I was one of the deputies took early retirement it occurred to me that I could become the head of the school. I felt as though I knew what needed to be done. I asked for advice from colleagues and friends. Much of it seemed to steer me away from the job. People would ask me, 'Have you applied for any other headships?' 'Why not start in a smaller school?' or simply, 'Are you sure?' I decided I was sure and so I took on the challenge and applied for the job.

I was successful and the day after I got the job was particularly strange. I knew I could do the job but was surprised that the interview panel had believed in me. I could also see the doubt on the faces of the staff, some parents and representatives from the education authority. During the morning I overheard a group of parents talking.

'Do you know who the new head is?'

'Yeah, it's some Indian woman.'

'No, it's not. It's Jasbir.'

That conversation brought home the enormity of the job to me but failure was not even going to enter the equation. Suddenly I was in a position to really make a difference. I have tried to list the most important things I have learnt since I became the head. I think they are, in no particular order:

- To be creative, on the lookout for opportunities to improve things. Education management for me is about stirring things up, getting people to think about what they are doing and why they are doing it.
- Just because something has been done in a particular way for the last 20 years doesn't mean you have to carry on doing it in the same way.
- Listen to what people, particularly children, have to say.
- Be incredibly organised. I surprise myself sometimes!
- Work with parents – they know what they want for their children.
- Have whole school policies that children have access and input into.
- If you don't like something, do something about it quickly.
- Flexibility and curiosity are essential ingredients. Flexibility is about developing new behaviours and patterns, about surprising yourself and other people, about extending your own limits. Curiosity is asking 'what if' questions.
- Celebrate successes, however small.
- Collect evidence of change.
- Be accessible to everyone – it is amazing what staff and children will tell you.
- Develop yourself and you will develop the children.
- Believe that problems have solutions.
- Don't change as a person. Keep hold of your fundamental beliefs and values.

On good days the job can be an opportunity for self-expression, personal as well as professional development and excitement. I think the most important message is that you don't have to be the head to bring about change. In fact, no change is possible without classroom teachers.

I recently received a letter which proved to me that some of the things I had worked for were paying off. The letter said,

Dear Jasbir,
(One of the dinner supervisors) has been making sexist remarks to the boys in Year 6 saying, 'Why are you playing with girls? Play with boys your own age,' and saying, 'Girls are allowed to play with small children because they're gentle and boys are rough.' We think that everyone should have an equal opportunity to play with little kids. We also think that the boys should and will learn to be gentle sometimes. We have been told we can't play in the bottom playground from Monday onwards. Please can you sort out our problem.

This letter was signed by four Year 6 girls and five Year 6 boys. They put the letter in the box I have outside my room for any pupil to write to me at any time. My first thoughts were of disappointment that this sort of incident would still happen and of confusion as to what to do with the member of staff. Yet the more I looked at the letter the more I realised that it actually showed our policies were working. These children had the skills to recognise various forms of discrimination: not only to recognise it but also how to react to them. The school may have a dining supervisor who doesn't understand its policies but it has children who understand them well. Our behaviour policy lists the following:

- We are all individuals with our own ideas and feelings.
- Everyone should be treated with courtesy and consideration and should receive respect.
- Everyone can set a personal example.
- Everyone should work and behave the best they can.
- We should praise and encourage each others' good points.
- We should be fair and consistent towards each other.
- We should only expect of each other what is reasonable and possible.

We expect both children and teachers to work towards these aims. The central purpose of this behaviour policy is to encourage good behaviour as opposed to punishing bad behaviour.

Teachers are responsible for ensuring that pupils are motivated to take part in their own learning and the assessing, reporting and recording of their own achievements. I am always delighted when a child brings a piece of work or a picture to show me – I give them one of my stickers and they march off to show their friends or anyone else who will look. We try to build in as many ways possible of recognising achievement – perhaps I remember not really knowing how well I was doing, not knowing how to measure success, and want to ensure my pupils do not feel the same way. We have special mentions assemblies, give out certificates, constantly change displays. Our aim is that by building upon achievement and planning the next stages with children we share with them what the learning criteria are and let them know what has been planned for them, what our expectations are. In this way we begin to give ownership of the learning to the learner. If we only value pupils for their outcomes and not the processes they go through in order to reach these outcomes we value only the tip of the iceberg and do not see the real power of education. Children are always learning – a good teacher can discover what it is that children are learning and work with it.

Reflection

You have read descriptions of a whole series of 'good' lessons. These lessons range from adult-based film workshops, through Open University tutoring to the lessons we can learn from the day-to-day life of the head of a primary school. A recent interview with a group of 12-year-olds helps sum up for us what all of these lessons had in common. They decided that a good teacher is someone:

- who puts the learner's best interests first;
- who doesn't change to impress other people;
- who tries new and different things;
- who is fair;
- who understands people;
- who can explain things without shouting;
- who explains things clearly;
- who teaches you things you don't already know;
- who doesn't shout when someone asks a question;
- who doesn't get grumpy;
- who lets you work together.

I think all of these qualities can be found in the lessons described above. Marc and Jasbir both describe ways of working in order to make discipline and control invisible and effective. Because both learners and teachers are excited about what is happening in the classroom and the possibilities for learning, the worry of indiscipline can disappear. Again, all of these lessons show teachers who have strong, caring relationships. They care passionately both about their work and the possible outcomes of this work. The teachers here talk to their pupils about learning and the aims for their lessons, not just about behaviour.

They seem to acknowledge that pupils should take as much responsibility as possible for their own learning – they allow control to pass from the teacher to the pupil. Most importantly they take care to make all pupils feel confident that they can do well and can achieve something worthwhile.

Questions for your journal

This time there are two sets of questions: one set dealing with your own best lessons and one exploring ways you may deal with frustrating situations in order to become a teacher who is 'good' in difficult and challenging contexts.

- What is your biggest success in terms of teaching someone else?
- What made this successful?
- What could you have done to make it an even bigger success?
- How do you know you were successful?

Secondly, here is a way to reflect on difficult pupils. Helen brought these ideas with her from a session run by a drama teacher called Geoff Gilham. Try to recall and write down a moment when you have been very frustrated either as a student/learner or with a student/learner. At this moment you were at a loss with how to deal with the situation. The following questions may help you deal with such situations, avoiding the feelings of shame, blame and failure and will help you avoid the temptation of rationalising such situations into invisibility, or simply seeing them as a confirmation of what you already know. By 'looking the animal in the eye' we are more ready to deal with similar situations in the future.

- What does the situation tell you about what it is like to be a young person at the present time?
- What does the situation tell you about the nature of society and the nature of the school?
- What does the situation tell you about your practice and about yourself?

Now look back on both the description you have written of the incident and the answers to the above questions.

- Which answers do you know to be accurate?
- Which answers do you think may be true?
- Which answers are simply hunches?

Now rewrite the incident changing the action so that it reflects what you wish had happened, and what you think was possible given the constraints at the time.

Part 4

What Makes a Good Education?

Chapter 8

Visions for the Future

My aim is to produce students who will leave school with the ability to look the world in the eye and say, 'I am me; here I am; this is what I can do: If you accept me then the world and myself will be enriched; if you reject me it is your loss as well as mine.'

R Ridley, Headteacher, Halifax High School writing in *Scottish Drama*, Issue 5 (1996)

This final chapter aims to draw together all the threads from our stories throughout the book. As an outcome to our discussion we focused on our vision for education to see if we could learn the lessons of our shared experience. We asked the questions, what is it to be an educated person? What sorts of teachers would this ideal person have had to support them in their journey, and finally, what kind of school would they have attended? What follows is the result of our final discussion.

What is an educated person?

In some ways this reads like an alternative checklist for school inspectors or perhaps the beginning of a National Curriculum which would support teachers interested not only in passing on a knowledge of their subject but also in developing the skills that all learners would exhibit if they had received an education in its broadest sense. We arrived at the list by brainstorming around the idea, 'An educated person ...'. This is the result.

- An educated person can learn independently; this doesn't mean that they sit on their own with a book. It means that they know they can learn if they put their mind to it, know how and where to find information and know how to involve others to help them learn. They can use educational skills they already have to work on new ideas. They are also excited about their learning and want to share their discoveries with others.
- An educated person doesn't simply blame the system and people within the

system for failures in their learning. They can pinpoint the problems and work to change things. They feel in control of their future and can work towards fulfilling their ambitions. They don't feel as though things just happen to them and that they have no power of choice.

- An educated person does not see people or subjects in stereotyped boxes, they see how individuals and groups work together to make the bigger picture, both inside and outside of school.
- An educated person is literate and numerate in the broadest sense. They use these skills to interpret the world around, to operate in this world and to create new possibilities for themselves and their communities.
- An educated person is fun to be with.
- An educated person knows that school can't teach you everything, they never stop learning and never stop wanting to involve others in that learning. They respond positively to change and are willing to take risks and take new directions in their lives that may look strange to others. They can learn from experience.
- An educated person knows their own strengths and weaknesses.
- An educated person is questioning and challenging. They know how and when to challenge others in order to make a positive difference. They also have a belief that they can make a difference in others' lives.
- An educated person can take exams and can pass exams. They understand the system and how it works. They have the skills and the confidence to play the system.
- An educated person has respect and trust for teachers who support them in their learning.
- An educated person retains a childlike excitement in the possibilities for the future. They are enthusiastic about new ideas and fascinated by new knowledge and skills.
- An educated person is open to influences and willing to change their mind, but does not simply just follow the crowd. They are not afraid to disagree. They keep an open mind and weigh up the options before committing to any one direction. They are honest and open about their idea.
- An educated person knows there are more questions than answers.

In your journal you may want to work with this list. Try to prioritise the list. Which do you feel are the most important and least important facets of an educated person? Pick the most important and the least important and write about why you have made this choice. Are there any statements you disagree with? Have we missed anything out?

What sorts of teachers can help develop an educated person?

Thinking through what makes an educated person stimulates us to ask, so what sorts of teachers have these educated people had? In what ways are they different from the teachers that exist at the moment. In some ways this is a development of the idea of teaching competencies which we described in the introduction to the book. So, in the same way that what is offered above is a development of the idea of a national curriculum as simply prescribed content, perhaps this list can be seen as a development of the present competencies that we expect new teachers to come to the classroom equipped with. In a book called *Action Research for Educational Change*, John Elliott offered an alternative list of competencies for teachers wishing to think deeply about what it is to teach. These competencies may be summarised as follows:

1 Knowledge and understanding of their subject

- An effective teacher can find common themes throughout many topics and can organise and communicate information in this way.
- An effective teacher can learn from reflection on their own experience, through observing their own behaviour and through observing the way others respond to their behaviour.
- An effective teacher can draw on a range of techniques from a wide variety of subject disciplines and use them appropriately in many different educational settings.
- An effective teacher can accommodate many different learning styles. Indeed, they value the diversity of experience within their classrooms.
- An effective teacher understands controversial issues in education, understands the tensions which are created in educational settings and works positively with these tensions.

2 Interpersonal skills

- An effective teacher shows positive regard for all fellow learners, and their carers.
- An effective teacher has the ability to give active support to fellow learners and colleagues.
- An effective teacher can control impulsive feelings of hostility and anger which would lead to making fellow learners and colleagues feel powerless and in-effective.
- An effective teacher has the skill to challenge antisocial behaviour appropri-ately. They know when to say 'no' to learners, their carers and colleagues.
- An effective teacher can see groups of learners and others as individuals and support their individual needs. They do not make blanket statements about 'parents' or '13-year-olds'.

3 Developmental skills

- An effective teacher takes risks which may lead to the development of new and original ideas.
- An effective teacher can set realistic, time-phased goals.
- An effective teacher is approachable and can use feedback from learners and colleagues to help them change and develop.
- An effective teacher uses a clear understanding of specific difficulties and problems to identify practical solutions which are seen as supportive by those experiencing the problems.

4 The ability to make a difference

- An effective teacher can create interpersonal networks which they use for support and development.
- An effective teacher can share goals with learners and colleagues and influence others by the creation of shared goals and a shared vision for the future.
- An effective teacher can see themselves as an agent of change and sees the possibilities of sustaining change through the development of collaborative networks.
- An effective teacher has an awareness of how power operates in and outside schools and understands how this affects the possibilities for change within the institution.
- An effective teacher values knowledge in others. They work to develop a powerful community not power over a community.

In your journal you may want to reflect on this list. Which qualities do you feel you already have? Which will you most need to work on? How can you develop these qualities and who will help you? What other qualities do you bring to the job of teaching? Why are they important?

Our vision of an achieving school

The final part of this chapter must then move from individuals to institutions. What sort of a vision do we have of the institution which houses these effective teachers and produces our image of an educated person? What we have below is our view of an achieving school. Of course the things that we are talking about are not as easily measured as the number of successes at A–C in GCSEs or what proportion of pupils are attaining level 4 in reading. The list does not deny the importance of these kinds of success criteria, we do however hope it adds an important dimension which is too often missed in the oversimplistic approach to ranking schools and pupils. Within this dimension, the value which is added to any league table is the valuing of the learner. So, in our achieving school:

- Pupils feel respected both as individuals and as part of an important and valued group within school.
- Pupils expect challenge through the activities offered in class and experience learning as a dynamic, engaging and empowering activity. They will experience this challenge in a supportive environment so that they are clear about the expectations placed upon them.
- Pupils expect to be treated fairly and will treat each other fairly and with respect.
- Pupils expect a developing autonomy as they progress through school, both as a right and as a responsibility.
- Pupils can rely on support from their teachers in relation to both academic and social concerns.
- Pupils expect to learn in security, relating both to the physical setting of the school and relationships with teachers and other pupils.
- Pupils can expect to leave school valuing learning as a way of developing control over their own lives. They will be equipped with the tools and qualifications necessary to make life choices which will enable them to participate fully in the variety of communities in which they live and which they help to create.
- Teachers expect personal and professional development and will accept responsibility to help colleagues develop.
- Teachers have a sense of achievement in their work and enjoy teaching.
- Teachers have the right to dignity and respect from each other and from pupils.
- Teachers expect recognition of their successes, from colleagues and from pupils.
- Teachers expect to work in an environment free from bias and discrimination.
- Teachers take an active role in decision making.

Let us take an imaginary walk through such an achieving school. As we enter the playground on our way to the school entrance the range of trees and plants catch our eyes. There are picnic tables where groups of pupils sit and chat as an alternative to joining in the playground games. Adults are engaged with the pupils – they seem to be enjoying this opportunity to spend time with the pupils out of lessons. We realise there is very little litter, probably due to the obviously placed litter bins. There is little vandalism or graffiti. In fact, what little damage there is is being tackled by a group of pupils working with the premises officer. The whole space seems to have been landscaped to provide quiet areas as well as large areas in which to play group games.

As we reach the entrance hall we are pleased to find that we can easily find our way in; the school is well signposted both externally and internally. We consult the photo board so that we know what the teacher we are looking for looks like before we meet them. It is nice to see the picture of the teacher working with pupils rather than simply a shot of her face. These pictures include several photographs of visitors to the school from the local community, sharing their skills with pupils and teachers and supporting the school. Our exploration of the notice boards which are covered with pupils' work and with statements from the school's mission statement is interrupted by the pupils on duty in the reception area who ask us to sign in, issue us with badges so that everyone in school knows we are official visitors and take us to the staff room whilst they go to find the teacher we have come to see.

As with the rest of the school the staff room appears to have been recently decorated: perhaps it is just well looked after. We realise the colour schemes are not the traditional institutional green or grey. We are impressed by the courses available to teachers, and by the report back from one of these courses on the staff notice board. Pinned next to this is the cycle of meetings all staff attend in school, working together to continually monitor and develop the curriculum they offer the pupils. The next of these is a meeting led by the mathematics co-ordinator who has just returned from a course exploring ways of supporting learners with special needs in mathematics. We also spend some time reading the reading policy on another board with suggestions by other staff for changes which need to be made. We do this fairly quietly so that we do not disturb the group of pupils in one corner. It appears as though they are a sub-group of the school council working on ways of developing a healthy tuck shop in school to help fund the further development of the environment outside the school.

The pupils on reception duty return and escort us to the teacher we are visiting. In the first room we pass through pupils are engaged in a science workshop, all gathered around separate tables engaged in a variety of experiments. In the next room an older child is leading a storytelling session with young children; they sit around her chair fascinated by the story she is telling. Our guides tell us that she has written it herself. Finally we pass through a room where the teacher is engaged in a whole class discussion, finding out what her class already knows about the history of the local area before they begin their next piece of work.

We arrive at the room we are visiting. We look for the teacher. At first we can't see her and then we realise she is sitting with a group of pupils having an excited conversation about something they have discovered. While we wait for her to finish with this group another group of pupils approach us because they are interested in the reason we are visiting the classroom. The teacher beckons us over and we go and sit in the corner of the room reserved for resources – it contains both computers and books and is obviously being used by pupils to carry out their own research.

. . . and so it goes on. Of course, all that you have read in this chapter is an ideal, a vision of an education system we would all be proud to work in and would all wish for our children. But it is an ideal created from fragments of teachers and

schools which already exist. You have read about such places in this book as well as the negative experiences which serve to sharpen our focus when we work to create our visions in practice. So our shared task is not to create something new from nothing but to work to bring together what already exists – a collaborative act of change.

Bibliography and Further Reading

This bibliography has been compiled from three sources. They are books which have particularly influenced the way we work or the way we see the learners we work with. That is why there are several novels in the list. The list also contains the books recommended by the tutors at the University of Nottingham for their student teachers. Finally those books which had a direct influence on the thinking of the authors as they wrote are included. These are the books by John Elliott, Lynn Davies, Jean Ruddock and Mary Louise Holly.

Bruner, Jerome. 1986. *Actual Minds, Possible Worlds*. Harvard: Harvard University Press.

Davies, Lynn. 1994. *Beyond Authoritarian School Management*. Education Now Books.

Donaldson, Margaret. 1987. *Children's Minds*. London: Fontana Press.

Elliott, John. 1991. *Action Research for Educational Change*. Milton Keynes: The Open University.

Griffiths, Morwenna. 1995. *In Fairness to Children*. London: David Fulton Publishers.

Hammond, Paul. 1974. *Marvellous Melies*. Gordon Fraser Books.

Holly, Mary Louise. 1989. *Learning to Grow*. London: Heinemann Books.

Holt, John. 1990. *How Children Fail*. Harmondsworth: Penguin Books.

Richardson, Robin. 1990. *Daring to be a Teacher*. Stoke on Trent: Trentham Books.

Rogers, Carl. 1994. *Freedom to Learn*. New York: New York Books.

Ruddock, Jean (Editor) *School Improvement: What Can Pupils Tell Us?* London: David Fulton Publishers.

Salinger, J.D. 1962. *Franny and Zooey*. London: Heinemann.

Scott-Baumann, Alison; Bloomfield, Alan and Roughton, Linda. 1997. *Becoming a Secondary School Teacher*. London: Hodder and Stoughton Educational.

Sutton, Clive. 1992. *Words, Science and Learning*. Milton Keynes: The Open University Press.

Syal, Meera. 1996. *Anita and Me*. London: Flamingo.

Walker, Alice. 1978. *The Color Purple*. London: Woman's Press.

Weber, Kenneth. 1978. *Yes, They Can*. Milton Keynes: Open University Press.